SMITHSONIAN INSTITUTION

NATIONAL AIR AND SPACE MUSEUM

SMITHSONIAN ANNALS OF FLIGHT
VOLUME 1 . NUMBER 4 . (END OF VOLUME)

AIRCRAFT PROPULSION

A Review of the Evolution Of Aircraft Piston Engines

C. Fayette Taylor

Professor of Automotive Engineering Emeritus
Massachusetts Institute of Technology

SMITHSONIAN INSTITUTION PRESS
CITY OF WASHINGTON • 1971

Smithsonian Annals of Flight

Numbers 1–4 constitute volume one of *Smithsonian Annals of Flight*. Subsequent numbers will not bear a volume designation, which has been dropped. The following earlier numbers of *Smithsonian Annals of Flight* are available from the Superintendent of Documents as indicated below:

1. The First Nonstop Coast-to-Coast Flight and the Historic T–2 Airplane, by Louis S. Casey, 1964. 90 pages, 43 figures, appendix, bibliography. Price 60¢.
2. The First Airplane Diesel Engine: Packard Model DR–980 of 1928, by Robert B. Meyer. 1964. 48 pages, 37 figures, appendix, bibliography. Price 60¢.
3. The Liberty Engine 1918–1942, by Philip S. Dickey. 1968. 110 pages, 20 figures, appendix, bibliography. Price 75¢.

The following numbers are in press:

5. The Wright Brothers Engines and Their Design, by Leonard S. Hobbs.
6. Langley's Aero Engine of 1903, by Robert B. Meyer.
7. The Curtiss D–12 Aero Engine, by Hugo Byttebier.

For sale by Superintendent of Documents, Government Printing Office
Washington, D.C. 20402 - Price $1.75

Contents

	Page
FOREWORD	VII
ACKNOWLEDGMENTS	VIII
EARLY ATTEMPTS AT PROPULSION	1
EARLY INTERNAL-COMBUSTION ENGINES	8
Wright Brothers' Engine 1903	9
Langley Engines 1900–1903	15
ENGINES 1903–1909	19
ENGINES 1910–1918	27
PISTON ENGINES AFTER 1918	35
Liquid-Cooled Engines	35
Air-Cooled Engines	41
Air Versus Liquid Cooling	53
UNCONVENTIONAL ENGINES	57
Barrel- or Revolver-Type Engine	57
Fairchild-Caminez Engine	57
Sleeve-Valve Engines	57
Diesel Aircraft Engines	59
Two-Cycle Gasoline Engines	60
Unconventional Cylinder Arrangements	62
RELATED TECHNICAL DEVELOPMENTS	63
Valves and Valve Cooling	63
Fuels and Combustion	65
Altitude Performance and Superchargers	67
Vibration Control	73
Propellers	75
Reduction gears	78
Other Developments	79
Ignition Systems	79
Carburetion	81
Fuel Injection	81
Starting	81
Bearings and Lubrication	82
Engine Instruments	83

SUMMARY OF PISTON-ENGINE DEVELOPMENT	85
Table 1—Engines of Historical Importance	88
Table 2—Credits, by Country, for Engine Developments	90
FOOTNOTES	91
APPENDIX—The Rotary Radial Engine	93
BIBLIOGRAPHY	95
(Expanded and arranged by Dr. Richard K. Smith, from material furnished by C. Fayette Taylor)	
Bibliographies and Indexes	95
History and Technology of Aircraft and Flight	96
(Publications primarily concerned with aircraft development, but incidentally containing valuable material on aircraft propulsion, or with theory and technological practice)	
Aircraft Powerplants	101
(Descriptions and technical data: under Engines, dates refer to date of publication)	
Aircraft Power Before 1900	101
Engines 1900–1913	101
Engines 1914–1919	103
Engines 1920–1924	104
Engines 1925–1929	106
Engines 1930–1934	108
Engines 1935–1939	109
Piston Engines 1940 and After	110
Steam Engines	112
Diesel Engines	112
Jet, Rocket, and Turbine Engines	113
Related Technical Developments	115
Altitude Performance and Supercharging	115
Cooling, Cowling, and Radiators	117
Carburetors, Carburetion, and Fuel Injection	118
Instruments and Accessories	119
(Engine instruments, fuel-supply and exhaust systems, ignition systems and spark plugs, starters and starting)	
Fuels and Combustion, Lubrication	120
Propellers and Propeller Gearing	121
National Advisory Committee for Aeronautics Annual Reports	123

Foreword

This, the fourth number of *Smithsonian Annals of Flight*, was the Fourth Lester B. Gardner Lecture, delivered at the Massachusetts Institute of Technology, March 8, 1962, and at the Smithsonian Institution, October 5, 1962. Subsequently it was published in the General Appendix to the *Annual Report . . . of the Smithsonian Institution . . . for the Year Ended June 30, 1962* (1963).

As presented here, the text has been revised, enlarged, and updated. Its 72 illustrations, many of them new, include a number of engines, aircraft, and the materials in the collections of the National Air and Space Museum.

With it, for the first time, appears the bibliography which accompanied the original manuscript and which, for lack of space, could not then (1963) be printed. This has since been edited and expanded to approximately double its original length by Dr. Richard K. Smith while he was serving on the Museum staff. Its nearly 600 entries, most of them contemporary accounts, cover the whole range of engine development and related activities from the early beginnings. This bibliography should be a useful and welcome tool, both for the airplane enthusiast and for the historian of aviation technology.

The active connection of the author, C. Fayette Taylor, with aircraft power started with his appointment in 1917 as officer-in-charge of the (aircraft) Power Plant Laboratory of the United States Navy, Washington, D.C. Here the engines of World War I, both foreign and domestic, were tested and improved. From 1919 to 1923 he was engineer-in-charge of the Power Plant Laboratory of the Army Air Service at McCook Field, Dayton, Ohio. Pioneer work on engines and fuels was done during this period. From 1923 to 1926 he was engineer-in-charge of design, and for a short while chief engineer at Wright Aeronautical Corporation, Paterson, New Jersey, concentrating on the development of air-cooled radial engines. Since 1926 he has been Professor of Automotive Engineering at the Massachusetts Institute of Technology, retiring from active duty there in 1965. He is still an active consultant in the field of internal-combustion engines.

Professor Taylor is author, with Charles Chatfield and Shatswell Ober, of *The Airplane and Its Engine* (McGraw Hill, 1928, 1932, 1936, 1940, 1948); with E. S. Taylor, of *The Internal Combustion Engine* (International Textbook Co., 1938, 1948, 1961); and of *The Internal Combustion Engine in Theory and Practice* (M.I.T. Press, Cambridge, Mass., 2 vols., 1960, 1968). He has also published numerous papers and articles in professional journals.

S. Paul Johnston, *Director*
National Air and Space Museum

July 1, 1969

Acknowledgments

This publication is based chiefly on the author's close personal connection with the development of aircraft engines during the period 1917–1950. Important editorial assistance by members of the staff of the National Air and Space Museum is gratefully acknowledged. Especial thanks are due to Mr. Robert B. Meyer, Jr., Curator, Propulsion. The bibliography has been edited and arranged by Dr. Richard K. Smith.

C. Fayette Taylor

AIRCRAFT PROPULSION

A Review of the Evolution
Of Aircraft Piston Engines

Figure 1.—Reproduction of Launoy and Bienvenue helicopter (NASM 1930–15), using bent-bow propulsion, 1784. (*Photo A–18232*)

Figure 2.—Pénaud's Planaphore (NASM 1930–17), using rubber-band propulsion, 1871. (*Photo A–19627*)

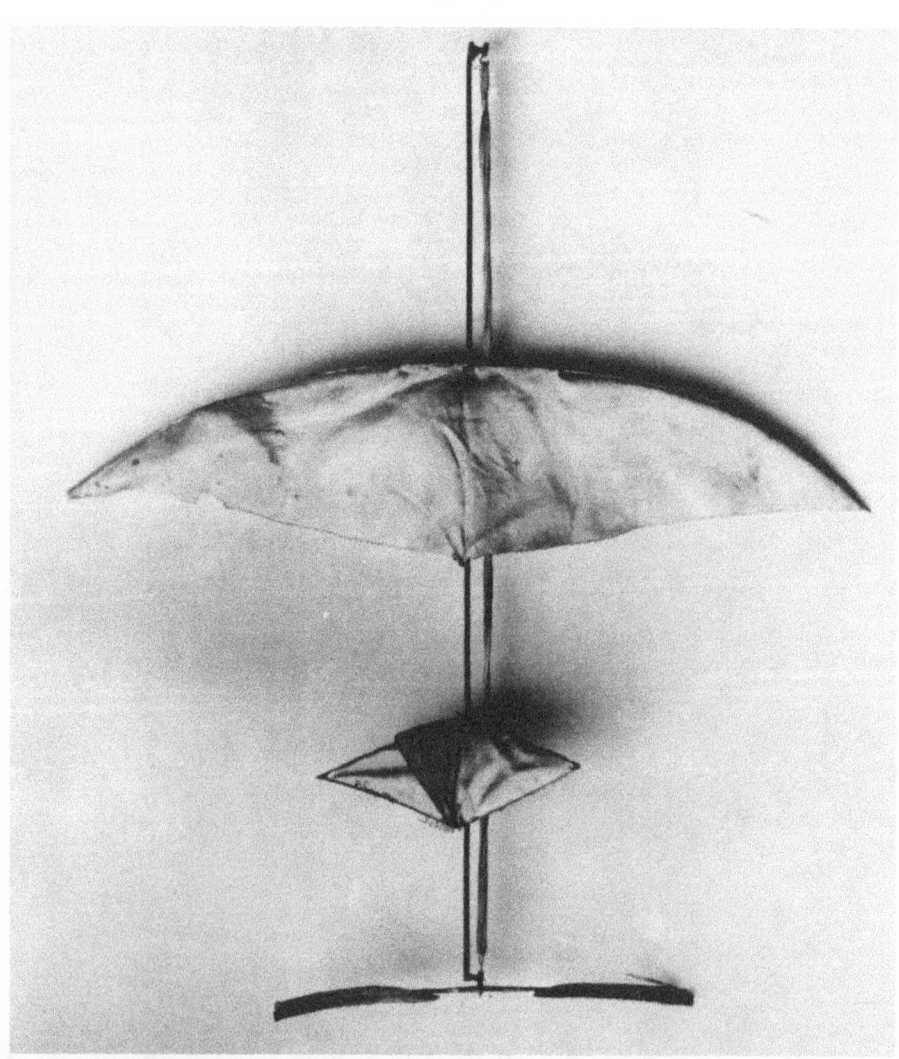

Early Attempts at Propulsion

MAN'S MUSCLES, USUALLY ATTACHED TO FLAPPING WINGS, were the earliest and most obvious source of power suggested for flight. In spite of innumerable attempts, there is no record of heavier-than-air sustained flight having been made with this kind of power until 1961, when Derek Piggot, in Hampshire, England, was reported to have flown 70 yards in a monoplane that was powered by a pedal-driven propeller.[1] On the other hand, many early balloons were equipped with oars or paddles, and at least two dirigible balloons, that of Charles E. Ritchel at Hartford, Connecticut, in 1878 and that of deLome in Paris, 1863, were equipped with propellers driven by pedals and a manned windlass, respectively. As late as 1907, Cromwell Dixon of Seattle, Washington, demonstrated a dirigible-airship powered by a pedal-driven propeller.

The first successful free flights by a man-made heavier-than-air contrivance seem to have been by model helicopters whose counter-rotating propellers, usually made of bird feathers, were driven by a wooden or whalebone bow (fig. 1). Charles H. Gibbs-Smith, in his excellent historical account *The Aeroplane*, credits the Chinese with this invention, as early as the 4th or 5th century, A.D. A French painting of such a device is dated 1460. Models of this type were flown by Launoy and Bienvenu in France in 1784, and by Sir George Cayley, "Father of Aerial Navigation," in 1792. Alphonse Pénaud (1851–1880) improved on Cayley's design by using twisted rubber bands, both for model helicopters and for a near-conventional model monoplane (fig. 2). This system of propulsion remains to this day the most important source of power for small airplane and helicopter models, and even today probably powers many more "airplanes" than any other type of powerplant. It is of historical interest to note that in the first detailed account of their pioneer flights the Wright Brothers attribute their early interest in flying to toy helicopters powered by rubber bands.

The first successful flight by a model airplane powered by means other than rubber bands is said to be that of Felix DuTemple in France, 1857–

NOTE: All footnotes are to be found on pages 91–92.

1858, using a clockwork motor. Steam power was later used by this same inventor, but there is no authentic record of successful flight. A compressed-air-driven model by Victor Tatin (France) made circular tethered flights in 1879.

Odd sources of power that have been proposed included tethered gryphons (birds were evidently considered inadequate), sails, and horses on a treadmill (obviously at least 1,000 pounds per horsepower). Some of these sources were even tried. The prize for ingenuity in the unconventional category might go to Portuguese reports, published about the year 1700, which described an aircraft sustained by magnets acting on electrified amber and propelled by a hand-power bellows blowing on its sails. Sir George Cayley built and tested a gunpowder engine in 1807, and in 1850 designed a model airplane powered by this means, but it was never built. A model ornithopter with wings operated by gunpowder, built by Trouve, is said to have risen from the ground in 1870.

There are records of two flights of dirigible airships using electric motors with batteries, namely, that of Tissandier at Auteuil in October 1883, and that of Charles Renard and Arthur Krebs near Paris in August 1884. The latter machine was considered quite successful.

Rocket power, inspired by the Chinese invention of the ballistic rocket in the 12th century, was suggested by Gerard in 1784. An English cartoon of 1825 shows a proposed rocket, propelled by a steerable steam jet, in flight to the moon. For man-carrying powered flight, the first use of rockets was by Fritz von Opel (Germany) in 1928. The first jet-engined flight was that of the Heinkel-178 airplane in Germany, 27 August 1939, powered with the HeS-3B gas turbine engine of 1,100-lb thrust, developed by Pabst von Ohain.

Steam power became a popular proposal for aerial navigation in the early 19th century, soon after it had been successfully demonstrated in ships, locomotives, and road vehicles. A model helicopter by W. H. Phillips (England) rose from the ground under steam power in 1842. Steam jets located in the wing tips were a remarkable anticipation of a modern application of jet power.

Contrary to most historical statements, the steam-driven airplane models of Henson and Stringfellow were apparently not capable of sustained rising or level flight. In the short indoor flights of record, take-off was from a horizontal wire somewhat higher than the landing point. Thus, these flights were what may be called "powered glides." The powerplants used are of interest, however, because of their advanced design. Gibbs-Smith attributes the powerplant design to Henson, stating that Stringfellow was

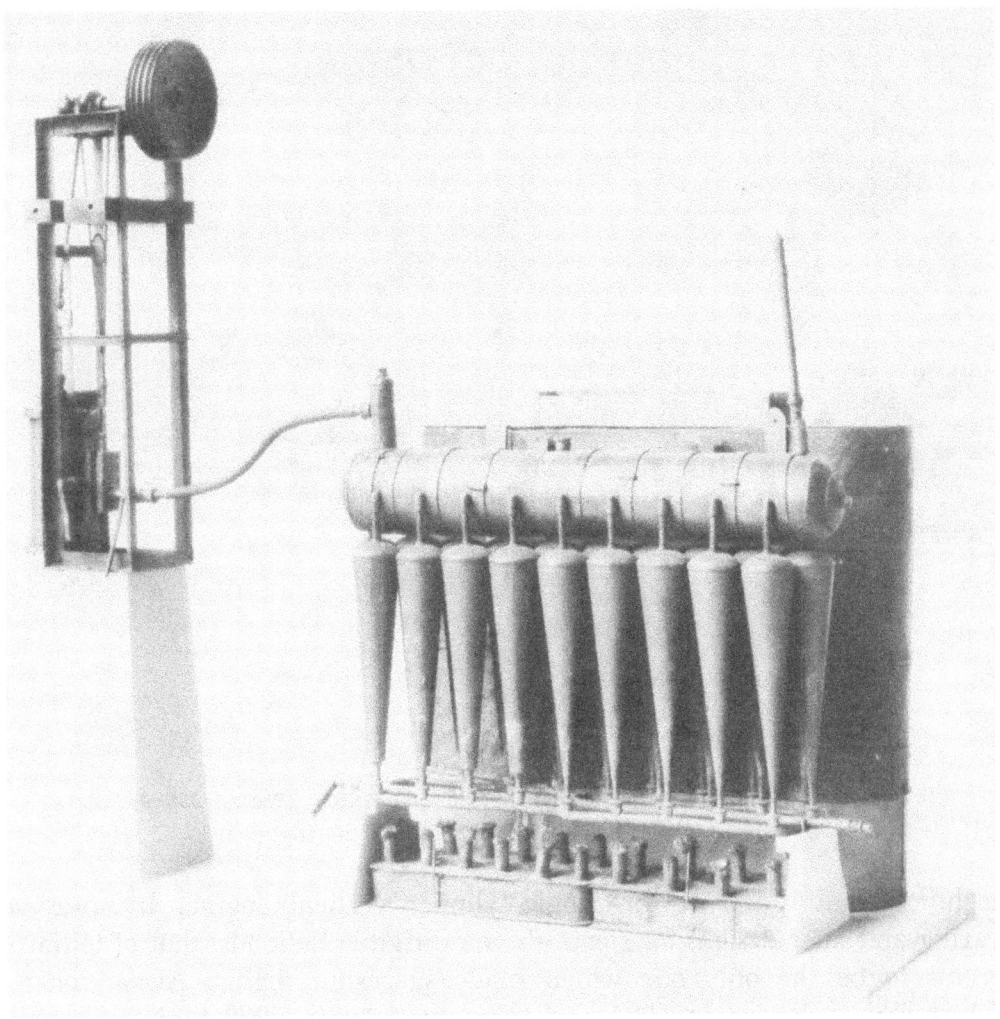

Figure 3.—Stringfellow engine and boiler (NASM 1889-1), 1868. *(Photo A-20030)*

more the skilled mechanic than the inventor. The 20-ft.-span model built by Henson but never flown was said to include a well-designed steam plant, but details are difficult to find. Stringfellow's "flying" model was a 10-ft-span monoplane equipped with a double-acting steam engine of $\frac{3}{4} \times 2$-in. bore and stroke driving two midwing 16-in. propellers geared to turn at three times engine speed. Its best powered glide was for about 120 ft indoors. A Stringfellow engine and boiler of 1868, a multibulb affair, is now at the National Air and Space Museum of the Smithsonian Institution (fig. 3).

A dirigible airship with a 3-hp steam plant weighing 351 lb was flown by Henri Giffard from Paris to Trappes in 1852 (fig. 4). I have not found a

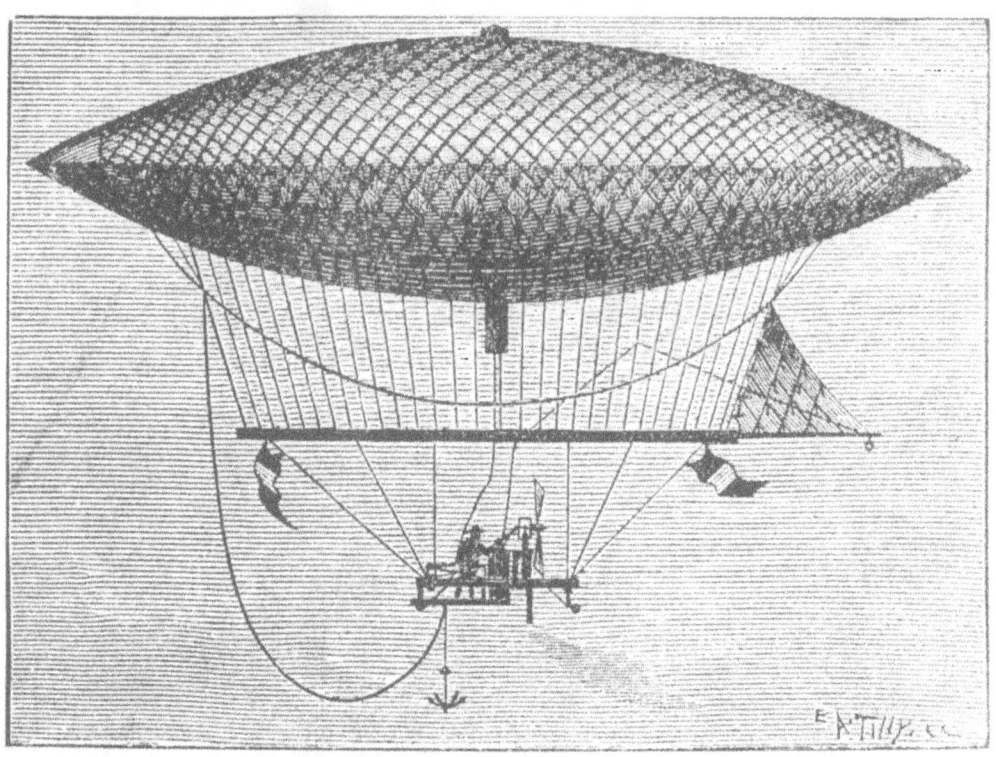

Figure 4.—Giffard airship, steam-engine powered, 1852. (Photo A-19889)

technical description of this single-cylinder vertical engine. In spite of earlier and later designs for steam-driven dirigible balloons, that of Giffard seems to be the only one which made successful flights. Alexander F. Mozhaiski in Russia in 1884 and Clement Ader in 1890 both built and tested full-scale steam-powered airplanes. At most, these machines made short uncontrolled "hops," although Ader's machine seems to have had the ability to lift itself without external assistance. No engine details seem to be available. The "Chauve-Souris," Clement Ader's "Avion III" of 1897, on display at the Conservatoire National des Arts et Metiers, Paris, France, is equipped with two 20-hp steam engines.

The best-known full-scale attempt at flight with steam was that of Sir Hiram Maxim in 1894. Maxim was an experienced steam engineer, and his powerplant was far more advanced than the aircraft to which it was applied. Its two twin-cylinder compound engines (fig. 5) each drove a pusher propeller. The powerplant was rated at 363 hp and weighed, complete, 1,800 lb, or 5 lb/hp, an extraordinarily light weight for its day. The boiler, (fig. 6) was of the multiple water-tube type, very much like

Figure 5.—Sir Hiram Maxim with his twin-cylinder compound steam engine, 1894. (*Photo A-42378*)

Figure 6.—Maxim's steam boiler, feed-water heater, and burner, 1894. (From *Journal of the Society of the Arts* (30 November 1894), vol. 43, p. 22.)

modern marine steam boilers. Operation along rails indicated that this engine could furnish the power necessary to lift even the monstrous contraption in which it was installed. Lack of success with this machine was not the fault of the powerplant.

Any discussion of steam power for aircraft should include the work of Dr. Samuel P. Langley, Secretary of the Smithsonian Institution, who built and successfully flew unmanned steampowered models [2] of 14-ft span in 1896. Fortunately, Langley's records are complete, and full technical details are available. The most notable feature of Langley's steam powerplants (fig. 7) was the use of "flash" boilers, that is, boilers consisting of one or more long coiled tubes with water pumped in at one end and steam issuing from the other. This type later was used successfully in the White automobile and is probably the type which would be used today if no alternative to steam power were available. Langley's steam plants weighed in the neighborhood of 7 lb/hp. He was perhaps the first to grapple with the problem of "flameout" in an aeronautical burner. A sentence from his memoirs reads in part, "Unfortunately there is a limit to this process [increasing the air flow through the burner] of increasing the air supply . . . a certain speed of efflux cannot be exceeded without putting the flame out." The early jet engines encountered this same problem.

Of course, steam ceased to be of importance for aircraft after flights by the Wright brothers and others had demonstrated the superior qualities of the internal-combustion engine, but it continued to have an emotional

Figure 7.—Steam engine used by Samuel P. Langley in his 14-ft-span Aerodrome No. 5 (NASM 1905-1), 1896. *(Photo A-12555)*

appeal to many people well into the 1930s. A Travelair biplane powered with a steam engine designed by William Besler was actually flown by the designer in California in 1932. A replica of this engine is in the Smithsonian's National Air and Space Museum (NASM 1965–253).

Steam was probably given the *coup de grâce* by Commander Eugene Wilson of the Navy Bureau of Aeronautics, a naval officer trained in steam power for ships, who reported in 1926, "On the basis of these three considerations [weight, economy, air resistance] they [steam powerplants] are absolutely impossible." My own opinion is not so extreme. If steam power was without competitors, we would have successful steam aircraft today, but at a considerable sacrifice in performance and perhaps also in safety.

Early Internal-Combustion Engines

The earliest successful aeronautical application of the internal-combustion engine appears to be in a dirigible-balloon flight by Paul Haenlein in Germany in 1872. A 4-cylinder 5-hp (40 rpm) Lenoir engine using coal-gas fuel was used. The Lenoir engine was the first commercial internal-combustion engine. The cylinders drew in air for half the stroke and fired at atmospheric pressure at midstroke. Efficiency was low—about 5 percent.

The relatively lightweight and relatively efficient "Otto-cycle" gasoline engine began with developments in England and Germany in the 1880s, stimulated by automobile development. Its application to aircraft came soon after. The first flight with this type of engine was apparently that of a dirigible airship designed by David Schwartz. The flight took place in Germany in 1897.

Alberto Santos-Dumont, in Paris in 1898, flew a dirigible equipped with a pair of "tricycle" engines in tandem, rated together at $3\frac{1}{2}$ hp and weighing, it is said, 66 lb, or 19 lb/hp. These engines were probably forerunners of the 3-hp Clement engine used by Dumont for his one-man dirigible airship flown during the summer of 1903. This engine was a 2-cylinder V-type, air cooled, and weighed 8.8 lb/hp. It is on exhibit at the Smithsonian's National Air and Space Museum (NASM 1908–1).

The first successful heavier-than-air flight powered by a gasoline engine was that of Langley's $\frac{1}{4}$-size model, which flew 350 ft on 18 June 1901, and 1,000 ft on 8 August 1903. The engine (fig. 8) was a 5-cylinder air-cooled radial, designed and built by Stephen M. Balzer and redesigned and rebuilt by Charles M. Manly. It produced 3.2 hp at 1800 rpm with a weight of 7 lb (see table 1, p. 88, for other data). At 2.2 lb/hp, this engine can legitimately be described as remarkable for its time. Figure 9 shows a letter from Manly giving some data on this engine that were not published in the *Langley Memoir*.

There is still some controversy, however academic and futile, about who made the first man-carrying powered flight. If short straight-ahead "hops" are counted as "flights," then the claims of Ader and Du Temple, pre-date the well documented flights of the Wright brothers in 1903. These

Figure 8.—Gasoline engine used in Langley's quarter-size model aerodrome (NASM 1950-3); 3.2 hp at 1800 rpm, 7 lb (without battery), 1901. (*Photo A-23759*)

were also short hops but they demonstrated good control and were followed soon after by sustained flights. Certainly the Wright brothers developed the first practical, controllable airplane; and their flights at Kitty Hawk, North Carolina, on 17 December 1903, mark the beginning of this revolutionary achievement. Also, the engine they used in 1903, and in their subsequent flights, was their own design.

The Wright engine of 1903, and the Langley full-scale engine completed late in 1901, and tested in 1902, 1903, and 1904, may be taken as the real beginning of the age of the reciprocating internal-combustion engine in aeronautics. As such, these engines are worthy of some detailed attention.

Wright Brothers' Engine, 1903

Little was known about the accomplishments of the Wright brothers until some years after their flights of 17 December 1903. Figure 10 shows a short and amusingly inaccurate report in *The New York Times* of 26 December 1903, which attracted little attention.

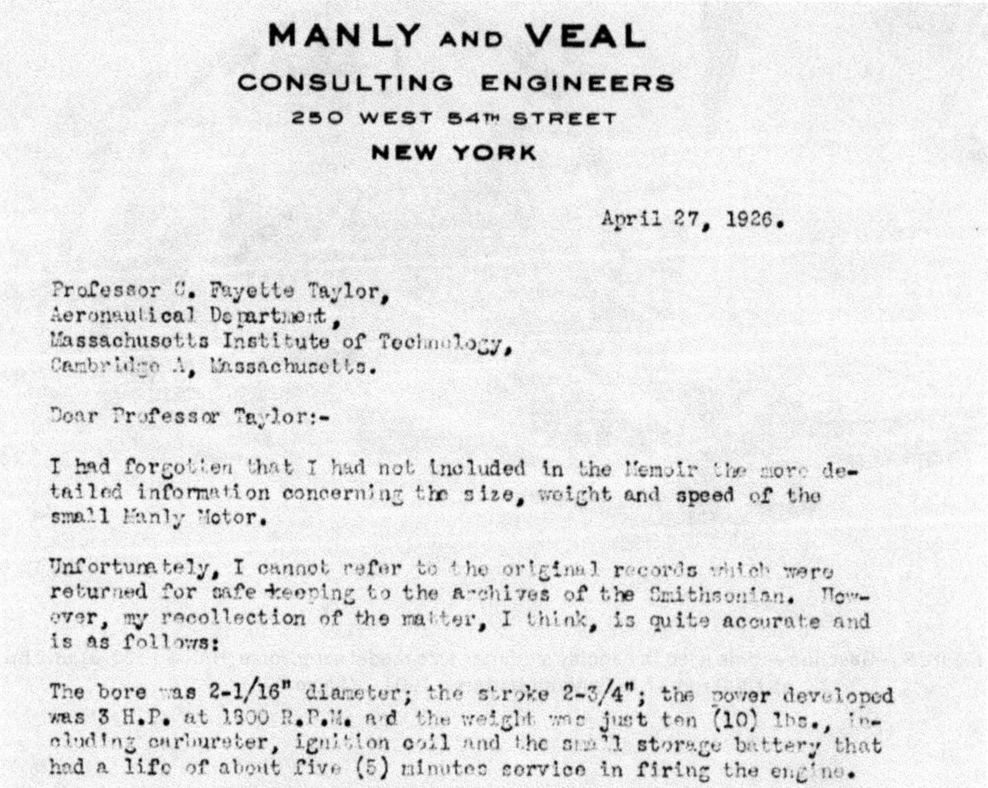

MANLY AND VEAL

CONSULTING ENGINEERS

250 WEST 54TH STREET

NEW YORK

April 27, 1926.

Professor C. Fayette Taylor,
Aeronautical Department,
Massachusetts Institute of Technology,
Cambridge A, Massachusetts.

Dear Professor Taylor:-

I had forgotten that I had not included in the Memoir the more detailed information concerning the size, weight and speed of the small Manly Motor.

Unfortunately, I cannot refer to the original records which were returned for safe keeping to the archives of the Smithsonian. However, my recollection of the matter, I think, is quite accurate and is as follows:

The bore was 2-1/16" diameter; the stroke 2-3/4"; the power developed was 3 H.P. at 1800 R.P.M. and the weight was just ten (10) lbs., including carbureter, ignition coil and the small storage battery that had a life of about five (5) minutes service in firing the engine.

I do not recall that any photographs were made of this engine except while it was assembled in the frame of the quarter-size model and believe that the pictures shown in the Memoir are as good as any that I had of it.

The cylinders of this engine were made of heavy steel tubing turned down to form thin integral radiating fins, with the cylinder barrel only 1/32" thick at the bottom of the fins. Castiron liners were shrunk into these cylinders and were bored out to leave them 1/32" thick. The cylinder heads were made from solid hand forgings (machined out) which were screw threaded and brazed to the steel cylinder barrels before the latter were finish machined. The general plan of construction of it was similar to that of the large engine except that it was air-cooled instead of water-cooled.

I will try to look up some personal memoranda that I have and see if I can give you more definite detailed data regarding the weight of the engine and its accessories, but, I think the above information is fairly accurate as to general features.

Yours very truly,

Chas. M. Manly

CMM/MCB

Figure 9.—Letter from Charles M. Manly describing the small gasoline engine of figure 8. (*Photo A-51010*)

AIRSHIP AFTER BUYER.

Inventors of North Carolina Box Kite Machine Want Government to Purchase It.

Special to The New York Times.

WASHINGTON, Dec. 25.—The inventors of the airship which is said to have made several successful flights in North Carolina, near Kitty Hawk, are anxious to sell the use of their device to the Government. They claim that they have solved the problem of aerial navigation, and have never made a failure of any attempt to fly.

Their machine is an adaptation of the box kite idea, with a propeller working on a perpendicular shaft to raise or lower the craft, and another working on a horizontal shaft to send it forward. The machine, it is said, can be raised or lowered with perfect control, and can carry a strong gasoline engine capable of making a speed of ten miles an hour.

The test made in North Carolina will be fully reported to the Ordnance Board of the War Department, and if the machine commends itself sufficiently, further tests will be made in the vicinity of Washington, and an effort made to arrange a sale of the device to the Government. The use to which the Government would put it would be in scouting and signal work, and possibly in torpedo warfare.

Figure 10.—Account of Wright brothers' first airplane in *The New York Times*, December 25, 1903.

In spite of the fact that the flights near Dayton in 1904 and 1905 were witnessed by numerous people, the press ignored them. The first eyewitness report published was a letter in *Gleanings in Bee Culture*, Medina, Ohio, 1 January 1905, by its publisher, A. I. Root, under the title "What God Hath Wrought." This article is reproduced by Gibbs-Smith in his book *The Aeroplane*.

An early public report by the Wrights themselves appeared in the September 1908 issue of *Century Magazine*, a publication similar in content and format to *Harper's* and the *Atlantic Monthly*. I recall discovering this article when our copy arrived at home, and I remember that my father, in spite of the many photographs of the machine in flight, refused to believe that human flight had been achieved. This attitude, five years after the Wright's first flight, was pretty general at the time, partly on account of the great number of false claims of flight which had been made in the past. These spurious claims also account for the seemingly incredible absence of reports by the Dayton press, whose representatives, after witnessing two unsuccessful attempts at flights made in 1904, failed to report eyewitness accounts of the many flights made in 1904 and 1905, or even to go eight miles out of town to see for themselves!

The *Century* article is extraordinary for its simple and beautiful expository style, and for its evidence of the almost excessive modesty of the brothers Wright, together with their rationality and persistence. I believe that it should be rated as a classic in American scientific literature.

The 1903 Wright engine (fig. 11) was designed by the brothers and built with the assistance of their faithful mechanic Charles E. Taylor (fig. 12; he is not related to the writer). This engine is especially well described by Robert B. Meyer in the *Annual Report of the . . . Smithsonian Institution . . . for the year ended June 30, 1961*. It was a 4-cylinder water-cooled, horizontal engine of 200-cu-in. displacement, with automatic inlet valves.

Figure 11.—Engine from Wright brothers' 1903 airplane (NASM 1961-48); 12 hp at 1090 rpm, 179 lb. (*Photos A-38626-B*)

Fuel was supplied by gravity from a small can on top of the engine. From there it flowed through an adjustment valve to a surface carburetor in the intake manifold, which was heated by the cylinder water jacket. Ignition was by a low-tension magneto with "make-and-break" spark contacts in the cylinders. The engine would give 16 hp for a minute or so, after which it gave a steady 12 hp. Control, such as it was, was by the spark timing. As shown in table 1, this engine was heavy and of low power compared to the contemporary Langley engine, but it flew! This basic design was later improved by the Wrights so that by 1910 it was delivering 30 hp for a weight of 180 lb, or 6 lb/hp.

The first and subsequent engines followed contemporary automobile practice in cylinder arrangement; however, crankcases were of cast aluminum, and the first engine had an en-bloc cast-aluminum water jacket. These, in use for aircraft engines from the beginning, have just recently come into use for some automobiles. After being in England for a number of years, the first Wright engine, with some alterations made subsequent to the 1903 flight, is now on display in the original airplane in the National Air and Space Museum, Smithsonian Institution.

Figure 12.—Wright brothers' mechanic Charles E. Taylor (left), who helped to build Wright 1903 engine, with a later model Wright brothers' engine. (From *Airway Age*, vol. 9, no. 12 (December 1928), p. 38)

Figure 13.—Langley Aerodrome A engine (NASM 1918-1), 1903, in test stand; 52 hp at 950 rpm, 135 lb. A description of this engine appears in "Langley's Aero Engine of 1903," by R. B. Meyer (*Smithsonian Annals of Flight*, no. 6, 1971). (Photo A-15864)

It was my good fortune to know Orville Wright, and to see him frequently during the period from 1919 to 1923 when I was engineer-in-charge of the aircraft-engine laboratory of the U.S. Army Air Service in Dayton, Ohio. He had previously retired from active participation in aeronautics, and had become a very modest, very quiet, much beloved member of the Dayton community, and of the famous Dayton Engineers Club.

Langley Engines, 1900-1903

Considering the state of the art at the turn of the century, the 52-hp 5-cylinder water-cooled radial engine Langley used in his Aerodrome represents one of the most remarkable pieces of engine design and construction ever achieved.

The history of this engine is interesting. In 1898 Samuel P. Langley, then Secretary of the Smithsonian Institution, had accepted a contract to develop a flying machine for the United States Government, and on June first of that year hired Charles M. Manly, a young graduate of Cornell University, as his assistant to supervise the design and construction of his Aerodrome. On 12 December, Langley contracted with a New York City automobile builder, Stephen M. Balzer, for a 12-hp engine to be completed in three months. Considering that even now, the development of a reliable gasoline engine is a matter of at least two years, this contract must stand as one of the most optimistic on record! Later, he contracted with Balzer for a 1½-hp engine to power a ¼-size model Aerodrome.

Neither engine had been delivered by 1900, and the slow progress led Langley and Manly to spend three months in Europe seeking even the prospect of an engine to power the full-sized Aerodrome. The search was unsuccessful and it was finally decided that Manly should join in the further development of the Balzer engines, which had failed to produce the power required.

These engines were of the rotating-radial type, but Manly, after further consulting European builders, decided to use the stationary radial principle. His choice was quickly justified. Whereas the full-scale rotary engine had developed only 8 hp and the small engine 1 hp, the first non-rotary versions produced 16 and 2 hp, respectively, an increase largely attributed to better valve action in the absence of centrifugal force. Further development resulted in the full-size engine of 1901, shown in figures 13 and 14, with specifications in table 1, and in the ¼-size one of the same year, described in Manly's letter of 27 April 1926 (fig. 9).

Both engines, described in detail in the *Langley Memoir*, are now displayed in the Smithsonian, removed from their Aerodromes. Power of the large engine was carefully measured on a dynamometer and, most remarkably, sustained for three consecutive 10-hr tests. The specific weight, 2.58 lb./hp,[3] remained as a low record until the Liberty engine of 1918. The figure 0.196-lb/cu in. displacement has never been closely approached.

The 5-in. bore cylinders, assembled by Manly himself, were built up of steel 1/16 in. thick, lined with 1/16 in. of cast iron.[4] The water jackets,

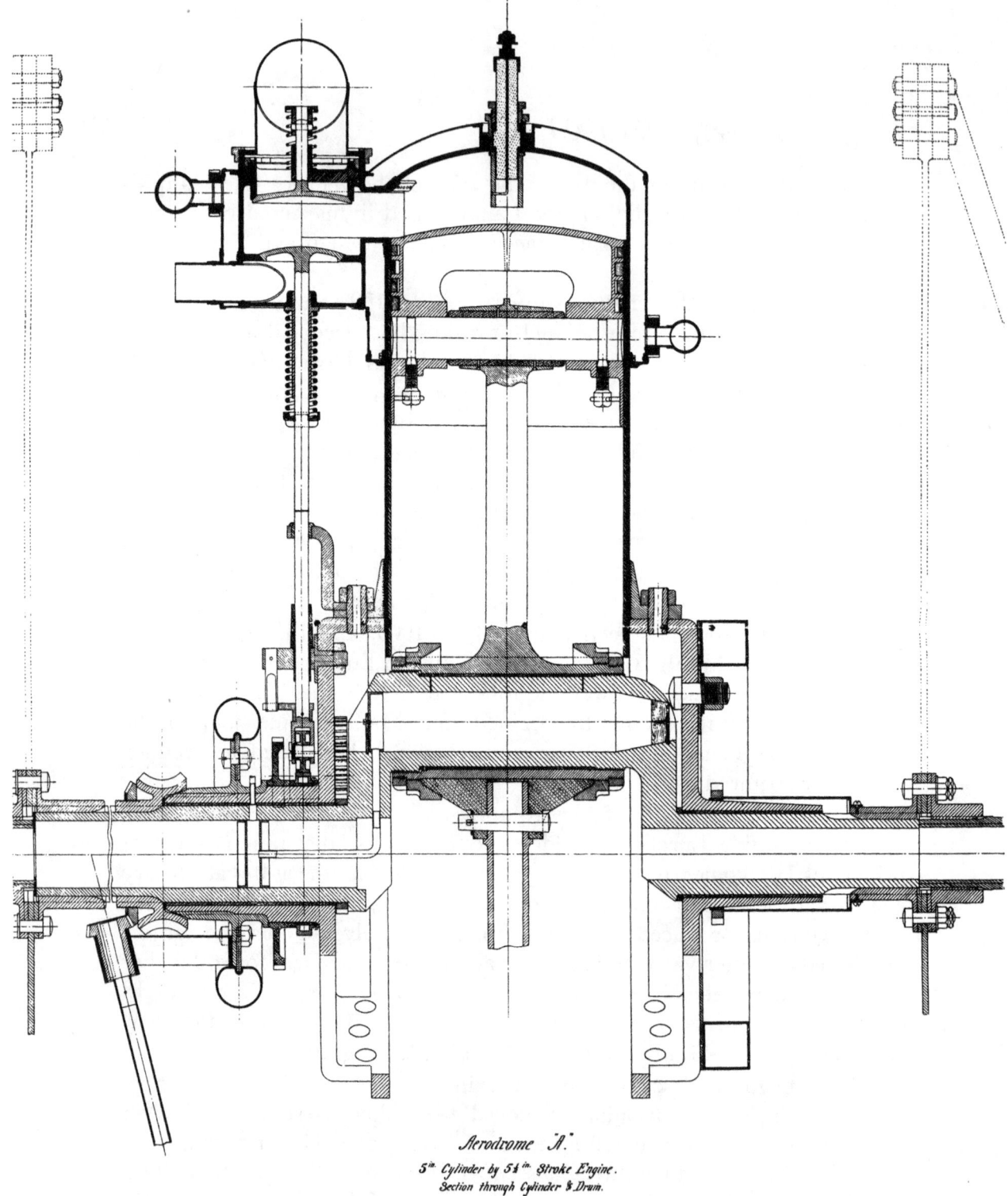

Figure 14.—Section through cylinder and crankcase of Langley Aerodrome A engine, 1903. (From *Langley Memoir*, pl. 78)

of steel 0.020 in. thick, were brazed onto the cylinder, as were the cylinder heads and valve ports. The difficulty of this operation is mentioned by Manly and can well be imagined.

This engine somewhat anticipated modern large aircraft engines in its use of the radial arrangement with a master connecting rod, its cam and valve-gear arrangement, and its use of crankcase, cylinders, and other parts machined all over to carefully controlled dimensions.

Manly's skill as an engineer and machinist was matched by his courage in making two (unsuccessful) takeoffs from the top of a houseboat, without previous instruction or experience as a pilot and in an airplane without landing gear. His survival of two crashes into the icy waters of the Potomac River testifies to his quick thinking and skill as a swimmer. In contrast to the poor preparation for the Manly attempts, the Wright brothers, before making their first powered flights, flew several hundred times in gliders of a size and type quite similar to that of their first powered airplane. All early Wright machines were equipped with landing skids.

Nowadays it is hard to appreciate the difficulties of these early aircraft-engine builders. Although successful automobiles were in operation both in Europe and in the United States, most of them were equipped with engines far too heavy and too low in power for airplane use. Accessory equipment such as spark plugs, carburetors, and magnetos was not available on the open market and had to be obtained from reluctant automobile builders or else built by hand. Worst of all, there was no established body of good practice, and details of existing practice were either very difficult to find or else held as closely guarded secrets. In view of these difficulties, the accomplishments of the Wrights and the Langley group are all the more remarkable.

Figure 15.—Antoinette monoplane with Levavasseur Antoinette engine, 1909. (*Photo A-3099*)

Figure 16.—Levavasseur Antoinette 8-cylinder engine, 1905–1907; 32 hp at 1400 rpm, 93 lb. (*Photo courtesy Science Museum, London*)

Engines 1903-1909

After the Wrights had demonstrated the actuality of airplane flight, a period of nearly three years elapsed before anyone else flew in a heavier-than-air craft. Meanwhile the Wrights increased their duration of flight to more than half an hour and their distance to nearly 25 miles, both records accomplished in their flight of 5 October 1905. In 1906 the Hungarian Trajan Vuia, the Dane J. C. H. Ellehammer, and the Brazilian Alberto Santos-Dumont accomplished flights, hardly more than short "hops," in airplanes with unconvincing control systems. Not until 9 November 1907, did anyone but the Wright brothers stay in the air for as long as a minute or fly a distance of over a thousand feet. On that date Henri Farman in a Voisin biplane flew 3,368 ft in 1 min 14 sec, with a 50-hp Antoinette engine, apparently under good control.

Antoinette engines (figs. 15 and 16) were built in Paris by Levavasseur as early as 1905 and were to become very important powerplants for European aviation in the next few years. Santos-Dumont used one rated at 24 hp for his "hop" of 772 ft in November 1906. The engines of Farman and Santos-Dumont were 8-cylinder V types rated at 50 and 24 hp, respectively. Farman's engine weighed 3 lb hp, a remarkable figure at that time (see table 1).

Antoinette engines had machined-steel cylinders with brass water jackets. All were water-cooled V types and were later built in 16- and 32-cylinder models. Together with the engines of Glenn Curtiss and the French ENV (fr., *en V*) of 1909, they pioneered the use of the water-cooled V-type engine in aeronautics. Other noteworthy details of the Antoinette included inlet port fuel injection, and evaporative cooling.

Louis Bleriot also used the 50-hp Antoinette engine in his first tractor monoplane, *No. VII*, which flew in December 1907. The first helicopter to lift a man off the ground (Paul Cornu, 13 November 1907) was also powered with an Antoinette engine. Cody made the first airplane flight in England on 16 October 1908 with an airplane somewhat resembling the Wright in design, powered by the 50-hp Antoinette.

The year 1908 was memorable for the rapid development of increasingly successful airplanes and engines. Two important new engines appeared—the 35-hp Renault 8-cylinder air-cooled V-type (an 80-hp example is shown in fig. 17) and the Curtiss air-cooled V-type 8-cylinder (fig. 18) which powered a flight of 1 min 43 sec in the *June Bug* on 4 July. And, except for Wright airplanes (which had flown for over an hour), the longest flight had been by Farman in a Voisin, 44 min on 2 October, until that day in 1908 that Wilbur Wright flew for 2 hr 20 min and 23 sec at Auvours, France. It was, according to a French commentator, *"un des plus passionants spectacles qu'ait présenté l'histoire des sciences appliqués."*

Glenn Curtiss was building and racing motorcycle engines soon after 1900. In 1902 Thomas Baldwin engaged him to supply an engine for Baldwin's dirigible airship, which flew successfully in 1904. In 1907 Curtiss joined the Aerial Experiment Association headed by Alexander Graham Bell, and thus began his distinguished career as designer and builder of both airplanes and engines and as an airplane pilot.[5]

Figure 17.—Renault 80-hp V-8 engine (NASM 1932–125), about 1916, with geared propeller drive (rating of the 1908 version was 35 hp at 1400 rpm, 242 lb). One of the earliest geared engines, it used long hold-down studs on the cylinders, a practice widely followed in later aircraft engines. (Photo A–42316–B)

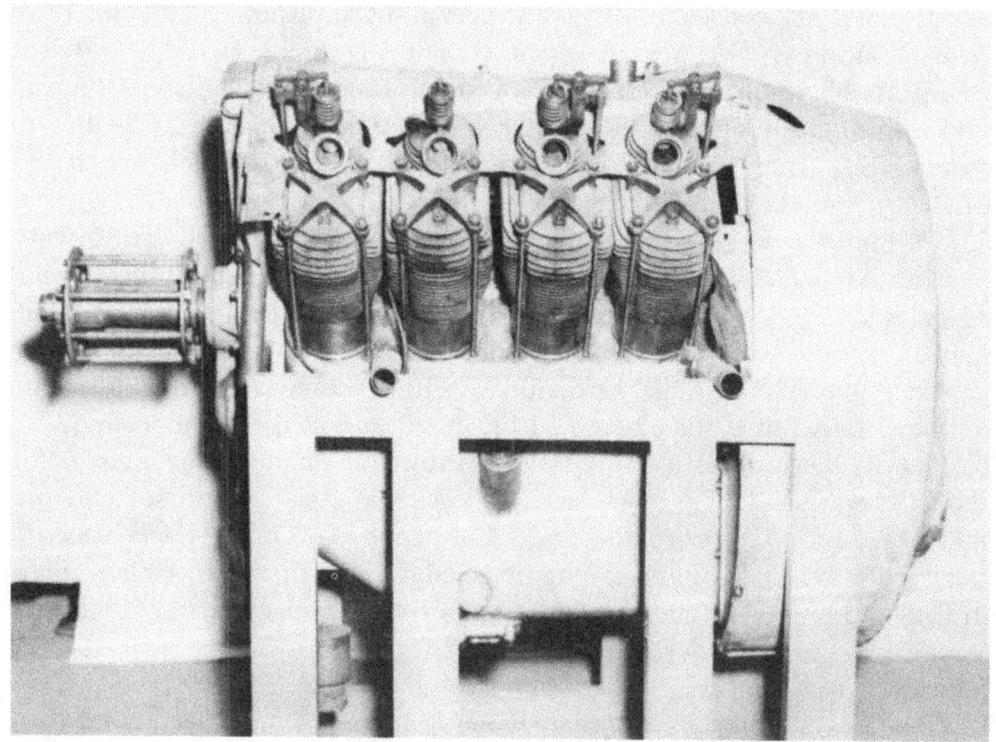

Figure 18.—(*Above*) Glenn H. Curtiss in his airplane *June Bug*, showing its 8-cylinder air-cooled engine installed, 1908. (*Below*) The *June Bug* at Hammondsport, New York. (*Photos A–3100, A–3101*)

Curtiss's earliest engines were air-cooled, including the V-8 engine used in the famous *June Bug*. Late in 1908, however, he settled on a water-cooled V-8 engine similar to the Antoinette of Lavavasseur except that the cylinders were of cast iron, with monel-metal water jackets.

Next to the Wright brothers, Glenn Curtiss was certainly the most important figure in early American aviation, both in engine and in airplane design. The most noteworthy engine which developed from his early work was the famous OX-5, to be described later. Engines bearing his name have an important place in aviation to this day.

The year 1909 has been called the "year of practical powered flying," because in that year flight began to be convincingly demonstrated by others than the Wright brothers. Four types of airplane—Wright, Antoinette, Farman, and Bleriot—had made flights of more than an hour's duration.

Bleriot made his famous cross-channel flight (37 min, 23.5 miles) on 25 July 1909. His tractor monoplane was equipped with a 24.5-hp 3-cylinder Anzani fan-type air-cooled engine (fig. 19). Later Anzani built 1- and 2-row radial air-cooled engines that were used in a number of airplanes prior to and soon after World War I. Another fan-type engine of this period was the REP of Robert Esnault-Pelterie, installed in an unsuccessful airplane in 1907. His subsequent REP fan-type engines were used in several successful airplanes.

An outstanding engine to appear in 1909 was the 50-hp 7-cylinder Gnome rotary-radial, first flown in Henri Farman's *No. III* biplane. Rotary types had been built for automobiles by Stephen Balzer and Adams-Farwell in the United States before the turn of the century, and this type had been originally planned and built for the Langley Aerodrome, but it was first adapted to flying in the Gnome. This engine (figs. 20 and 21, table 2, p. 90) was a masterpiece for its time and deserves special attention here.

The design of the Gnome was by Laurent Seguin. Made entirely from steel forgings machined all over, with integrally machined cooling fins and a modern master-rod system, it anticipated many features of the latest large air-cooled radials. The rotary feature was used in order to eliminate the flywheel, which had been previously thought essential, and also to assist in cooling. It frequently used a cowling with central air intake, something like that later developed for static radials by the National Advisory Committee for Aeronautics (see p. 90). Unlike the NACA cowling, however, the cowling used here had its opening for outlet air at the bottom, rather than around the rear edge. Its primary purpose was, probably, to

Figure 19.—Anzani 3-cylinder fan-type engine, 1909. The type used in Bleriot's crossing of the English Channel, its rating was 24.5 hp at 1600 rpm, 145 lb. (*Photo A-49846-E*)

encourage discharge of exhaust gases and oil *under* the airplane, away from the pilot. The fact that it also greatly reduced engine "drag" as compared with uncowled engines, may not have been understood at that time. This seven-cylinder model, and subsequent larger and more powerful versions, became perhaps the most popular aircraft engines up to World War I and were used widely by both sides through that war.

I had the pleasure of flying with a Gnome engine in 1920 and found it exceptionally free of vibration and also relatively quiet.[6] The only disagreeable feature was the castor-oil fumes discharged from the exhaust. Lubrication was achieved by pumping castor oil into the crankshaft at a

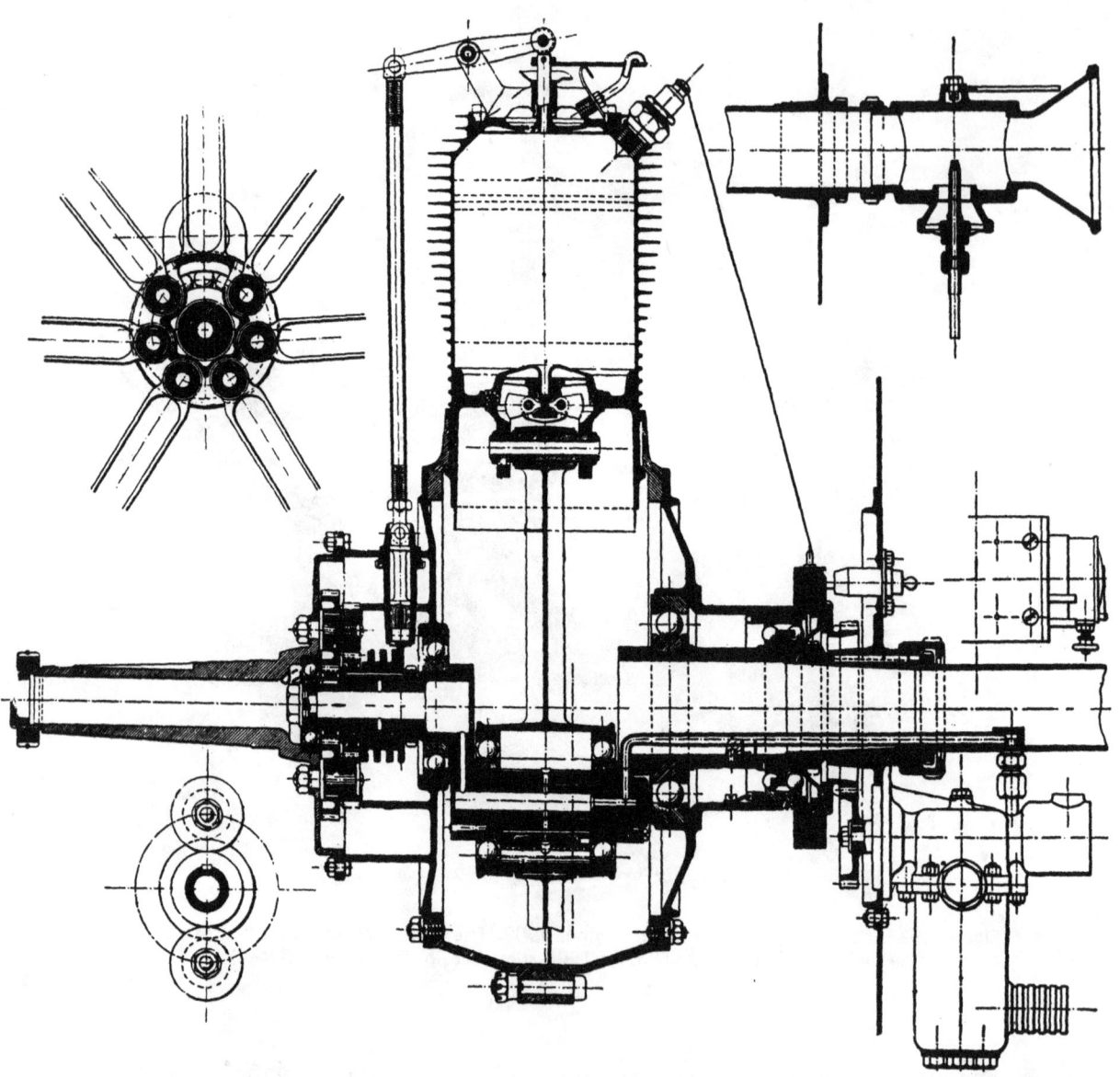

Figure 20.—Gnome 7-cylinder Monosoupape rotary-radial engine, 1910; 50 hp at 1150 rpm, 165 lb. In this longitudinal section note inlet valve in piston to admit fuel-air mixture from crankcase. (From *Aerosphere 1939*, p. 341)

Figure 21.—Gnome 50-hp 7-cylinder rotary engine, 1910, as installed in Gressier Canard pusher biplane. (*Photo A-50895*)

fixed rate, and oil which was not burned eventually found its way out of the exhaust ports and, despite the cowling, much of it settled on the airplane (and on the pilot!). One of my first assignments in aviation (1917) was to make tests to show that mineral oil could be used in aero engines. Previous to that time castor oil had been considered as indispensable for aero engines as it was for young children.

Another interesting feature of the Gnome engine was its method of control. No carburetor was used; the fuel and air were introduced through the hollow crankshaft, by means of separate valves controlled by the pilot. Because of the great inertia of the rotating engine, it was possible to adjust to the appropriate mixture by trial, without danger of stalling the engine. With a known setting of the valves for idling, after the engine had been started the air throttle was opened wide, at which time firing ceased but rotation continued. The fuel valve was then opened until firing restarted and maximum propeller speed was attained. Because the reverse process was difficult, throttling down was accomplished by temporarily cutting the ignition, and the engine was kept going by short bursts of power. Oddly enough this technique was easy to learn and pilots seemed to like it.

Important engines of 1909 included the following (see also table 1, p. 88).

Wright	4- and 6-cylinder vertical, water cooled
Curtiss	8-cylinder V-type, water cooled
Antoinette	8- and 16-cylinder V-type, water cooled
ENV	8-cylinder V-type, water cooled
Darracq	2-cylinder opposed, water cooled
Gnome	7-cylinder rotary, air cooled
Renault	8-cylinder V-type, air cooled
REP	7-cylinder fan, air cooled
Anzani	3-cylinder fan, air cooled

These engines accounted for nearly all important flights in 1909, including the winners of the first official aviation contests at Rheims.

The Darracq engine, used by Santos-Dumont, was important for being one of the first aircraft engines to use mechanically operated inlet valves. The JAP (J. A. Prestwich Co.) motorcycle engine used by A. V. Roe in his early airplane appears to have been the only other one using such valves. All other aircraft of the period used automatic inlet valves, opened by suction. Since automobile engines had been using mechanically operated valves for many years before 1909, it is hard to understand, why this important feature was so late in coming into use for aircraft engines.

Engines 1910-1918

The period 1910–1918, which included World War I, saw such rapid developments of aircraft engines that only the important ones can be described here. By "important" I mean those which pioneered successful new design features or which were particularly notable in service.

Early in this period the Gnome air-cooled rotary engine was dominant and was built in many countries and in several modified designs, including models by LeRhone and Clerget (French) the Bentley BR–1 and BR–2 (British) and the Oberürsel and Siemens (German). It reached its maximum development early in the war and was definitely obsolescent by 1918. Reasons for its demise were chiefly a limitation on speed due to centrifugal stress, the considerable windage losses, design limitations imposed by rotation of all parts but the crankshaft, and a rather strong gyroscopic effect on the airplane during turns. It set a pattern, however, for the later development of the modern air-cooled radial engine. It was a forged-and-machined-all-over engine, and it was radial and air-cooled, features which are now characteristic of most large aircraft piston engines. Other rotary engines were built at this time, but none achieved the importance or success of the Gnome and its descendants.

As the rotary engines became obsolete, the water-cooled V-type engine became dominant. In the United States the Curtiss OX–5 engine (fig. 22 and table 1, p. 88) led the field until 1917, when the Liberty and Hispano-Suiza engines were introduced.

The OX–5, a water-cooled V–8, had an aluminum crankcase, cast-iron cylinders (see fig. 34a) with sheet monel-metal water jackets brazed onto the barrels, and overhead valves, push-rod operated. Used by both Army and Navy, it powered practically all United States and Canadian training airplanes and was probably responsible for training more pilots for World War I than any other engine. The best-known trainer, the Curtiss JN–4, affectionately known as the Jenny, is shown in figure 23. My first airplane ride (1917) was in a single-float seaplane with the OXX–2, the Navy version of this engine.[7]

Figure 22.—Curtiss OX-5 water-cooled V-8 engine (NASM 1920-8), 1917; 90 hp at 1400 rpm, 320 lb (see also fig. 34a). *(Photo A-1832)*

Figure 23.—Curtiss JN-4 Jenny airplane with OX-5 engine, 1915. *(Photo courtesy Harrah's Automotive Museum, Reno, Nevada)*

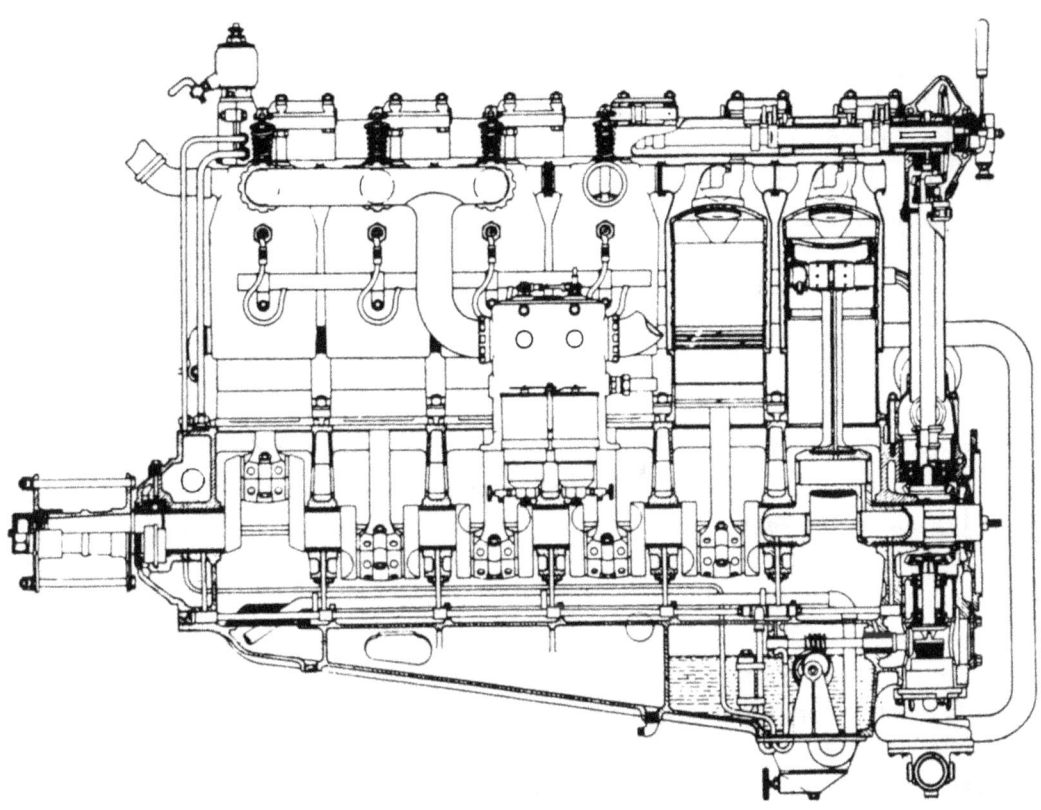

Figure 24.—Mercedes 6-cylinder engine, 1915; 180 hp at 1500 rpm, 618 lb. This engine pioneered welded-steel cylinder construction. (From [British] Ministry of Munitions, *Report on the 180-H.P. Mercedes Engine*, March 1918)

Figure 25.—Rolls-Royce Eagle V-12 engine, 1917; 360 hp at 1800 rpm, 900 lb. Its cylinder construction is similar to that of the Mercedes in figure 24. (*Photo A–487*)

The OX-5 engine was considered very reliable for its day, but few pilots completed the training course (very short) without at least one forced landing. Its weaknesses included single ignition, a rather flimsy valve-operating gear including "pull-rods" for the inlet valves, and a tendency to leak water from the water pump down onto the low-slung carburetor. In freezing weather the latter defect accounted for many forced landings

A very important new style in liquid-cooled cylinder design appeared in 1915 on the German 6-cylinder 180-hp Mercedes engine (fig. 24 and table 1, p. 88). This was the built-up welded-steel cylinder construction widely used for a long time thereafter in most water-cooled engines. It was copied by such famous makes as the Rolls-Royce Eagle (fig. 25), Liberty, FIAT (Fabrica Italiana Automobili Torino), Renault, Salmson, and BMW (Bayerische Motoren Werke), but finally gave way to the cast-aluminum en bloc construction, to be discussed later (p. 33).

Among the engines built in this style, an important one was the United States Liberty (figs. 26, 27, and 34b), which was developed under extraordinary circumstances.[8] After a decision on 29 May 1917 (only 7 weeks after the United States entered the war), by the War Production Board to build an airplane engine more powerful than any in use up to that time, J. G. Vincent, Chief Engineer of Packard, and Elbert J. Hall, of the Hall-Scott Motor Co., started to design such an engine in the Willard Hotel, Washington, D.C. On 31 May preliminary layouts were approved by the WPB and some extra help was called in. Complete layouts were approved 4 June, all drafting was completed by 15 June, the first 8-cylinder engine was delivered to the Bureau of Standards for test 3 July, and the first 12-cylinder engine completed the official 50-hr test 25 August 1917. The first "production" engine was delivered to the Army Air Service in Dayton on Thanksgiving Day 1917, just 6 months after Vincent and Hall had started their layout. I believe this record has never been equaled, before or since, except perhaps by the first Pratt & Whitney Wasp, described later.[9]

The design was based on the welded-cylinder construction pioneered by Mercedes. It had no radical features, but was an excellent synthesis of the state of the art of its time. Its principal weaknesses were cracking of the cylinder-head water jackets, burning of exhaust valves, and breaking of accessory gears. These faults were gradually reduced as time went on, and it came to be considered a reliable engine. Early production engines had a 50-percent chance of passing the government 50-hr endurance test. In later modification a bar was welded between the ports to reduce cylinder

Figure 28.—Wright Aeronautical Corp. Hispano-Suiza Model E V-8 engine, magneto end, 1920; 180 hp at 1700 rpm, 470 lb. The French-built model was rated at 150 hp (see also fig. 34c). (Photo A-51011)

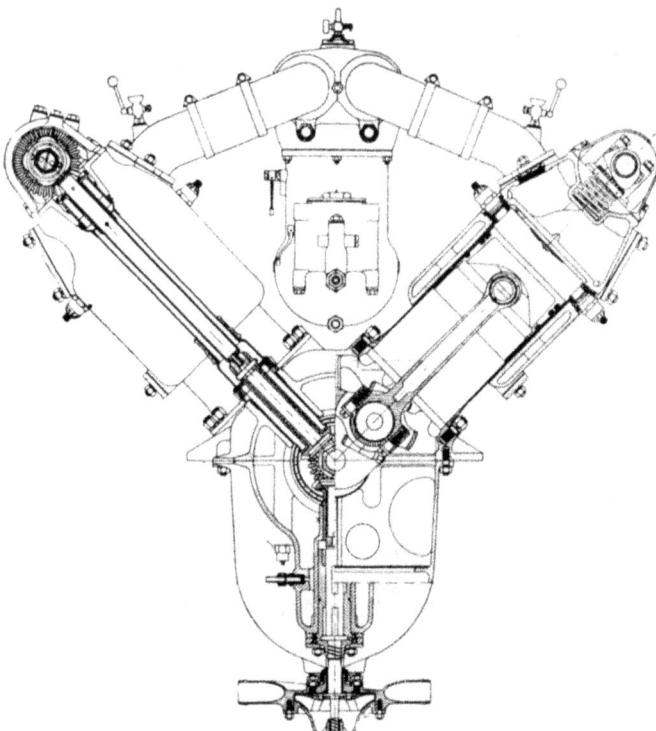

Figure 29.—Hispano-Suiza V-8 engine, transverse section, viewed from rear. (From *The French Hispano-Suiza Aero Engine, Instruction Book*, p. 25)

Figure 26.—Liberty V-12 engine, 1918; 420 hp at 1700 rpm, 856 lb. It has Mercedes-type cylinder construction (see also fig. 34b). (*Photo A-691*)

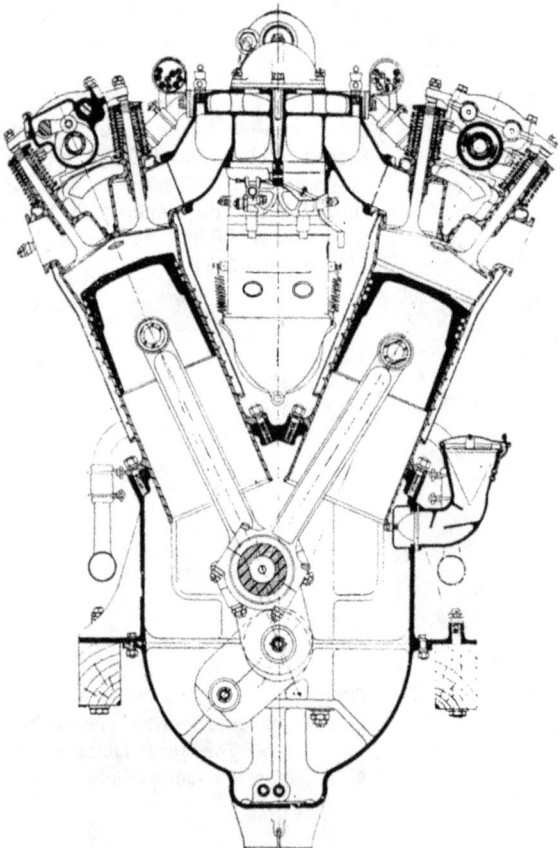

Figure 27.—Liberty 12A, V-12 engine, transverse section viewed from rear, 1918. (From *Aerosphere 1939*, p. 467)

distortion and jacket cracking, and heavier teeth were used in the gears. The only major weakness remaining was in the exhaust valves, which served well most of the time.

Large quantities of the Liberty-12 engine were produced by the automobile companies, including Packard, Ford, Lincoln, and some General Motors divisions. It was used by the British in military airplanes as well as by the United States Army Air Service and Naval Flying Corps. Liberty engine production was far ahead of airplane production in this country, and at the end of the war many thousands of these engines were on hand. Many were sold at low prices to "rum runners" and were very successfully used in running liquor through the Coast Guard blockade along the Atlantic and Pacific coasts during the Prohibition Era. During these years the Coast Guard had no "requirements" for a light and powerful marine engine, and their motor boats were far outclassed by the Liberty-equipped bootleggers' craft.

The Liberty engine remained important in United States Army and Navy aviation well into the 1930s. This engine was used in the NC flying boats with a special economical carburetor setting developed at the Washington Navy Yard. The NC-4 was, of course, the first aircraft to cross the Atlantic, 16–27 May 1919.[10] The Liberty was also the first engine to fly nonstop across the American Continent (in the Fokker T-2, 2–3 May 1923, piloted by Kelly and McCready).[11] Also, in a turbo-supercharged version, it held the world's altitude records in 1920, 1921, and 1922, and in 1924 it powered the flight of several Army airplanes around the world.

From a technical viewpoint, the outstanding airplane engine during World War I was undoubtedly the Hispano-Suiza V-8 (figs. 28, 29, and 34c, and table 1, p. 88), built first in Barcelona by a Swiss engineer, Marc Birkigt. It was adopted for French fighters in 1915 and used in the Spad (Société pour Aviation et ses Dérivés) 7 and 13, perhaps the best fighters of World War I (see fig. 30).

The basic contribution of Birkigt to engine design was the en bloc cylinder construction with a cast-aluminum water jacket containing steel cylinder barrels and with enclosed and lubricated valves and valve gear.[12] The success of this engine started a revolution in liquid-cooled engine design which culminated in the Rolls-Royce Kestrel and Merlin, via the Curtiss K-12, C-12, and D-12 engines. It was also the prototype for the Mercedes and Junkers engines which were the backbone of the 1940–45 German Luftwaffe, together with en-bloc Russian, Japanese, and Italian designs. By 1917 Hispano-Suiza engines were being built in England and the United States, as well as in France.

Figure 30.—An Hispano-Suiza V-8 powered this Spad 7 airplane, used by 27th Squadron, AEF, World War I, 1917–1918. (*Photo A-44832-C*)

The only weakness in the early Hispano-Suiza engines, by standards of the time, was a tendency toward exhaust-valve burning. This was due to the fact that the steel cylinder heads were "dry," that is, they did not come directly into contact with the cooling water (see figs. 29 and 34c). The flat steel head had a tendency to warp and lose contact with the aluminum jacket, which reduced valve cooling and also distorted the valve seats, causing exhaust valves to leak and burn under conditions of severe operation.

The development of this engine was continued in the United States after World War I by the Wright-Martin Company, which in 1919 became the Wright Aeronautical Corporation. One of the most important changes made was to eliminate the steel cylinder head and to seat the valves in bronze inserts pressed into the aluminum heads. This basic improvement set a pattern for the most successful subsequent liquid-cooled engines. In contrast to the all-forged construction of the Gnome and the modern large radial engines, the Hispano-Suiza engine and its descendants were essentially cast-aluminum engines except for the moving parts and the cylinder barrels.

Piston Engines After 1918

In the period after 1918 hundreds of new engine types appeared. From the technical point of view, the period is marked by the following significant developments:

> Further development of the liquid-cooled engine of the all-cast type, chiefly for military purposes
>
> The development of the air-cooled radial engine to a place of dominance in all but fighter-type military and small civilian aircraft
>
> The advent of 4-cylinder vertical in-line, and later, opposed-cylinder, horizontal, air-cooled engines for light aircraft

Liquid-Cooled Engines

By 1920 the success of the Hispano-Suiza engines, then built in both the original and a larger (300 hp) size had convinced most designers that the welded-cylinder construction was obsolescent.

The Curtiss Company in the United States took up the cast-aluminum engine, generally based on the Hispano-Suiza, with successive 12-cylinder designs known as the K–12,[13] C–12, D–12 (fig. 31), and V–1400 models. These were all of the 12-cylinder V-type, with 4 valves per cylinder, instead of 2 as in the Hispano-Suiza. The two early models had steel cylinder heads like that of the original Hispano-Suiza, but cooling was greatly assisted by an integral stud, in the center between the valves, by means of which the head was held tightly against the water-jacket casting (fig. 34d). In the D–12 the steel head was abandoned, and the valve seats were bedded directly in the aluminum head, as in the Wright version of the Hispano-Suiza.

The great success of the Curtiss engines in racing (first to exceed 200 mph in the Mitchell[14] Trophy race, Detroit, 1922, and winner of the Schneider trophy in 1923 and 1925) led the Rolls-Royce company to develop aluminum V–12 engines of similar type. The first was the Kestrel

Figure 31.—Curtiss D-12 V-12 engine; 325 hp at 1800 rpm, 704 lb. This engine was the first to fly more than 200 mph, in the Mitchell Trophy race, Detroit, 1922; and for the race, engine speed was increased so that it probably developed about 400 hp. (*Photo A-3109*)

Figure 32.—Rolls-Royce Merlin 61 V-12 engine with 2-stage supercharger, about 1944; 2000 hp at 3000 rpm, about 1700 lb. (*Photo A-3110*)

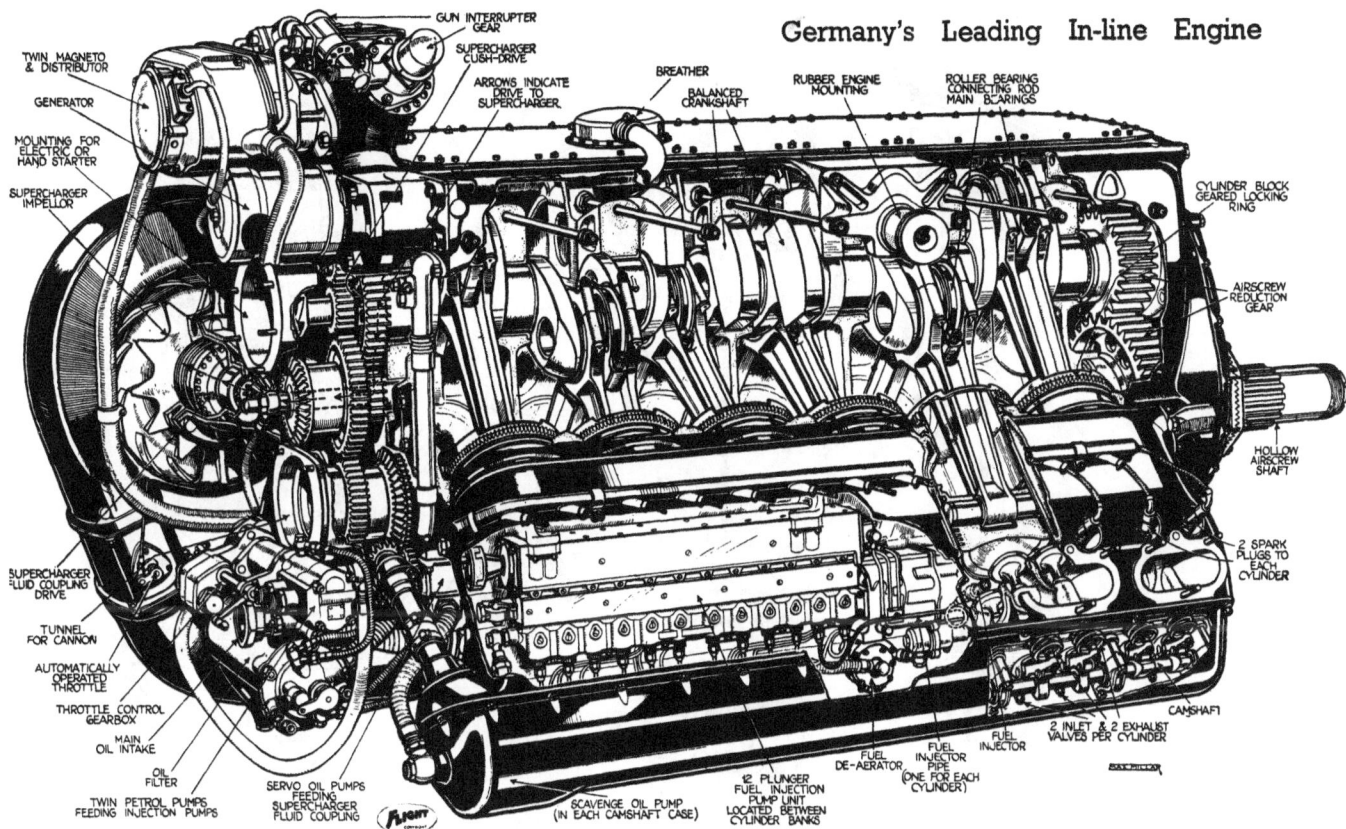

Part-sectional drawing of the liquid-cooled D.B.601N of 33.9 litres, bore and stroke 150 × 160 mm. Features of the engine are the twelve plunger in-line direct injection pump, and the fluid coupling which provides an infinitely variable gear for the supercharger drive. B.H.P. at 2,600 r.p.m. is 1,270, which for a weight of 1,540 lb. = 1.20 lb./h.p.

Figure 33.—Daimler-Benz, DB-601-N V-12, Germany's leading World War II engine (see also fig. 34h). Roller bearings are used on the crankpins. (From *Flight*, vol. 41, p. 367, April 16, 1942.)

of 1927 soon followed by the racing, or R, type which attained theretofore unheard of power output in proportion to its size and weight and won the Schneider trophy in 1929 and 1931. The Kestrel was followed by the Rolls-Royce Merlin (fig. 32), winner of the Battle of Britain, and also by the Allison V-1710 (a fairly faithful copy of the Merlin), and the German Daimler-Benz (fig. 33) and Junkers V-12 liquid-cooled engines, all descendants of the Hispano-Suiza and Curtiss. In all these engines the valves were seated in inserts embedded in the aluminum head, and thus had better valve cooling than the original Hispano-Suiza design. In every case the basic structure consisted of cast aluminum crankcase with en bloc water jackets and cylinder heads, also of cast aluminum. Cylinder barrels were uniformly of steel. Design details varied, especially in the method of taking the cylinder-head-to-crankcase load. This was successfully done as follows (fig. 34 illustrates the evolution of liquid-cooled cylinder construction):

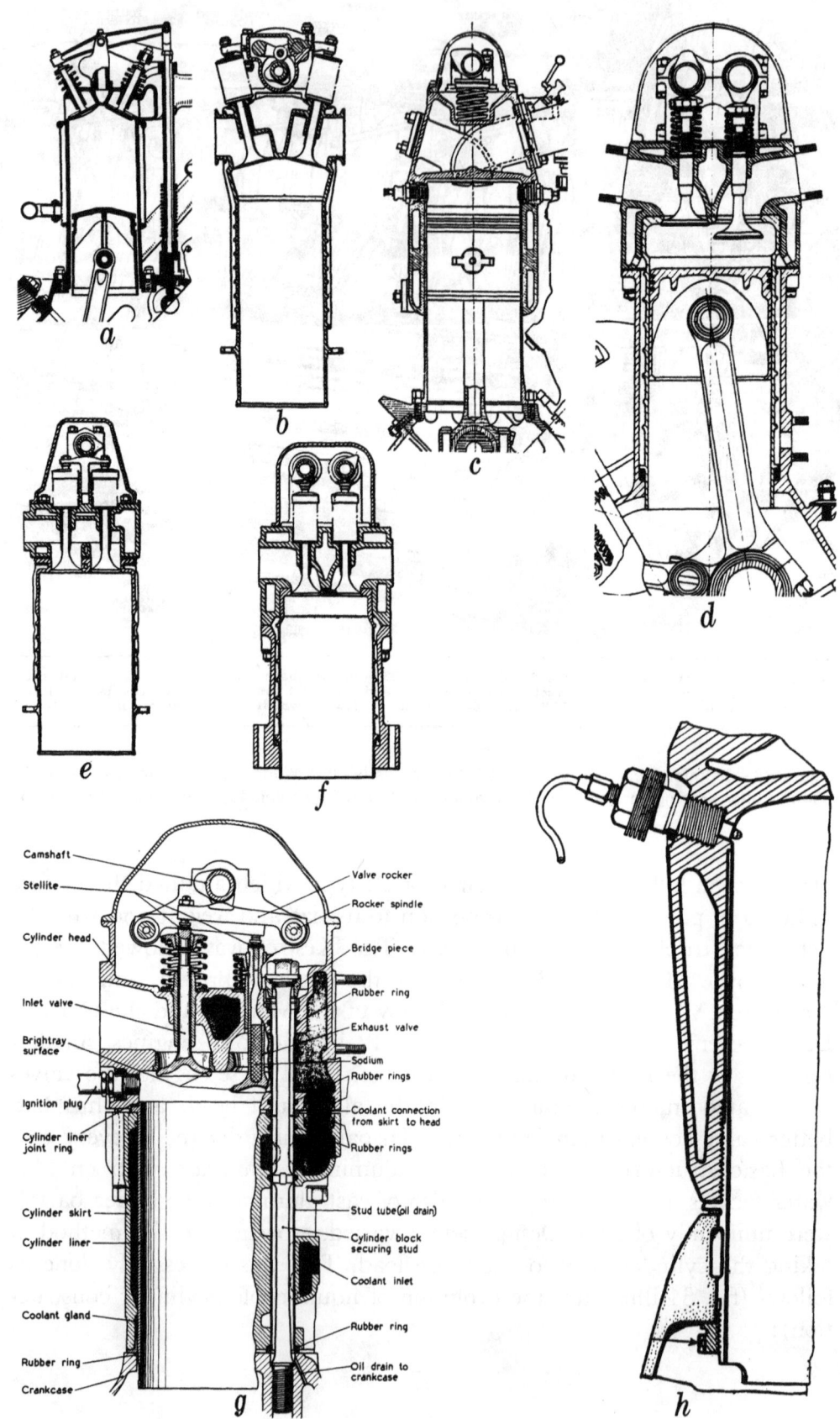

Through the cylinder barrels—Liberty (fig. 34b), Hispano-Suiza (fig. 34c), Packard (fig. 34e), and Daimler-Benz (fig. 34h)

Through the aluminum water-jacket structure—Curtiss (fig. 34d and f) and Junkers V-12 gasoline engine

By long bolts from cylinder heads to crankcase—Curtis OX-5 (fig. 34a), Rolls-Royce (fig. 34g) and Allison

The improvement in performance of liquid-cooled engines since 1918 has been astonishing. The following figures for two engines of nearly the same piston displacement and representing design ideas 30 years apart illustrate this development:

	1918	1948
Engine	Liberty	Packard Merlin
Number of cylinders	12	12
Bore and stroke, in.	5x7	5.4x6
Maximum hp	420	2,250
Rpm	1,700	3,000
Brake mean effective pressure, psi	118	360
Mean piston speed, ft-min	1,985	3,000
Hp per sq in. piston area	1.78	8.2
Weight, lb, per hp, dry (without water, oil, radiators)	2.04	0.78

Figure 34.—Liquid-cooled cylinder development:

	Year	Name	Barrel	Jacket	Load by
a	1914	Curtiss OX-5	Cast iron	Monel sheet	Studs
b	1917	Liberty	Steel	Steel, welded	Barrel
c	1915	Hispano-Suiza	"	Cast aluminum	"
d	1921	Curtiss K-12 [1]	"	" "	Jacket
e	1922	Packard V-12 [2]	"	Steel, welded	Barrel
f	1923	Curtiss C-12 [3]	"	Cast aluminum	Jacket
g	1934	Rolls-Royce Merlin	"	" "	Studs
h	1935	Daimler-Benz [4]	"	" "	Barrel

[1] Water jacket is cast integral with crankcase.

[2] Aluminum casting containing valve ports and camshaft was continuous over 6 separate steel cylinders.

[3] Improvement on K-12 by bolting separate water-jacket casting to crankcase for easier assembly and disassembly.

[4] Unique fastening of cylinder barrels to crankcase by means of a ring nut.

These improvements are attributable not only to improved detail design, but also to important developments in fuel, supercharging, and cooling fluid, which will be discussed later.

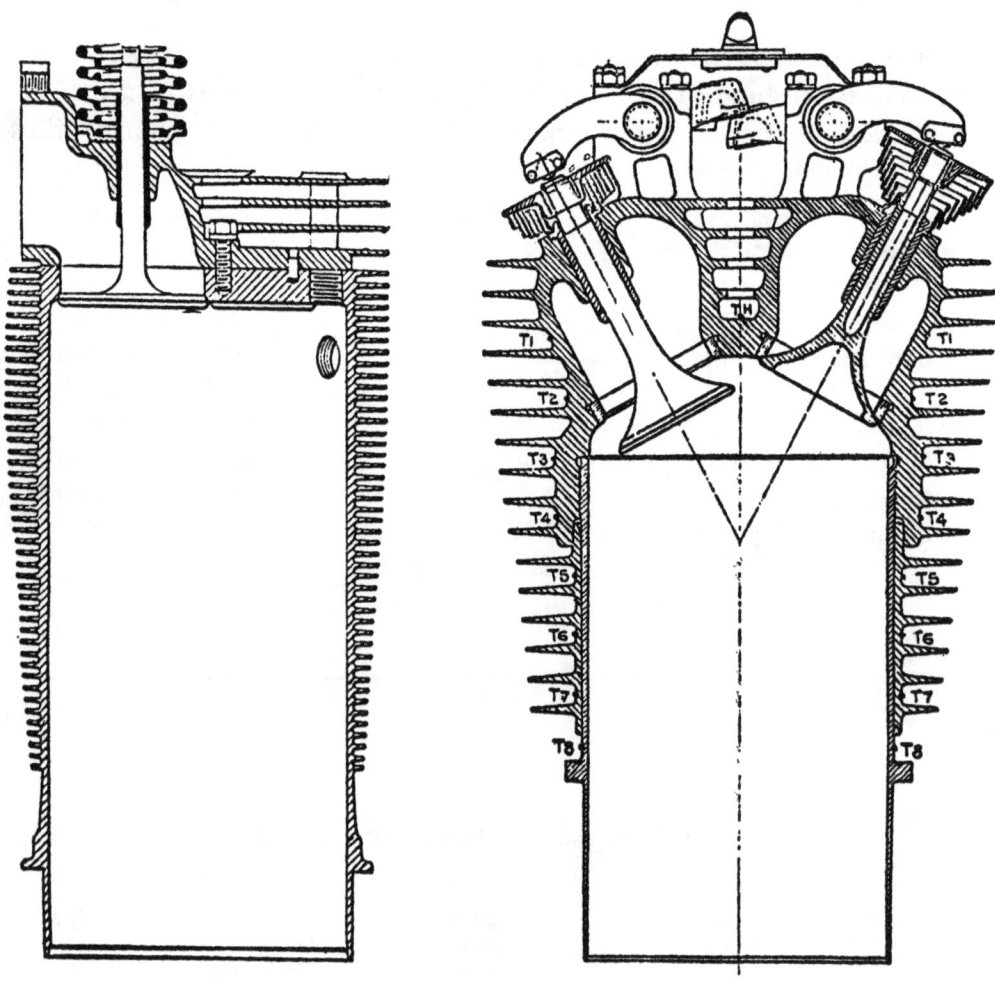

Figure 35.—British air-cooled cylinder development: *Left,* ABC steel cylinder with finned aluminum cap, 1917; this cylinder had poor head and valve cooling (from *Journal of the American Society of Naval Engineers,* vol. 38, no. 4, p. 872, 1926). *Right,* Cylinder developed by Dr. A. H. Gibson at Royal Aircraft Establishment, 1918, anticipated the essential features of modern air-cooled aircraft-engine cylinders—that is, aluminum head, with hard valve-seat inserts, screwed over steel barrel; applied finning on barrel is typical of many modern engines (from [British] Advisory Committee for Aeronautics *Report I.E.C. 260,* p. 268, fig. 11, January 1919).

Air-Cooled Engines

The Gnome and its rotary descendants (LeRhone, Clerget, Bentley B. R., Oberürsel, and others) were obsolescent by 1918. Also obsolescent were air-cooled engines using cast-iron cylinders with integral heads and fins. These included the radial Anzani, and the Renault V-type with its descendants, the RAF (Royal Aircraft Factory), and FIAT.

During the first World War it had become evident that the simple cast-iron cylinder[15] had reached its limit, and the Royal Aircraft Factory of Great Britain had employed Prof. A. H. Gibson, assisted by Samuel D. Heron, to develop more effective air-cooled cylinders. By 1918 they had constructed and tested steel cylinders with cast-aluminum heads screwed onto them, that were capable of higher specific outputs than any cast-iron cylinder (fig. 35, right). However, the practical use of the aluminum-head cylinder in England was seriously delayed by a parallel development, starting in 1917, of air-cooled radials with steel flat-head cylinders capped by a bolted-on valve-port assembly of cast-iron or cast aluminum (fig. 35, left). This cylinder design suffered from the same trouble as the early Hispano-Suiza engines, namely, poor exhaust-valve cooling because of poor contact between the head and the separate cooling element; however, the first radial engine using this cylinder type, the ABC (All British Engine Company) Wasp of 4½-in. bore, was successful enough to gain the support of the British government for its development in a larger version, the Dragonfly of 5½-in. bore. The fact that cooling problems increase with increased cylinder size evidently was not realized at the time.

This development finally became, through several changes in ownership, the Bristol Jupiter engine (fig. 37), which was built and used in considerable quantities in England and in Europe, chiefly for military purposes. It was never a really satisfactory aircraft engine, because of poor exhaust-valve cooling (S. D. Heron said that its consumption should be given in terms of pounds of exhaust valves, rather than in pounds of fuel, per horsepower-hour!). Finally realizing this fact, Bristol changed from steel heads to Aluminum heads with the Jupiter F, about 1930.

Meanwhile the Gibson-Heron type cylinders had been further developed by Armstrong-Siddeley, and were used on the Jaguar 2-row radial (fig. 38) which passed its type test in 1922, ten years after Gibson started his work.

A parallel development of air-cooled engines with aluminum cylinders having steel liners was begun about 1916 by Charles L. Lawrance. Starting with a 2-cylinder opposed engine, he built a 3-cylinder engine in 1919, and

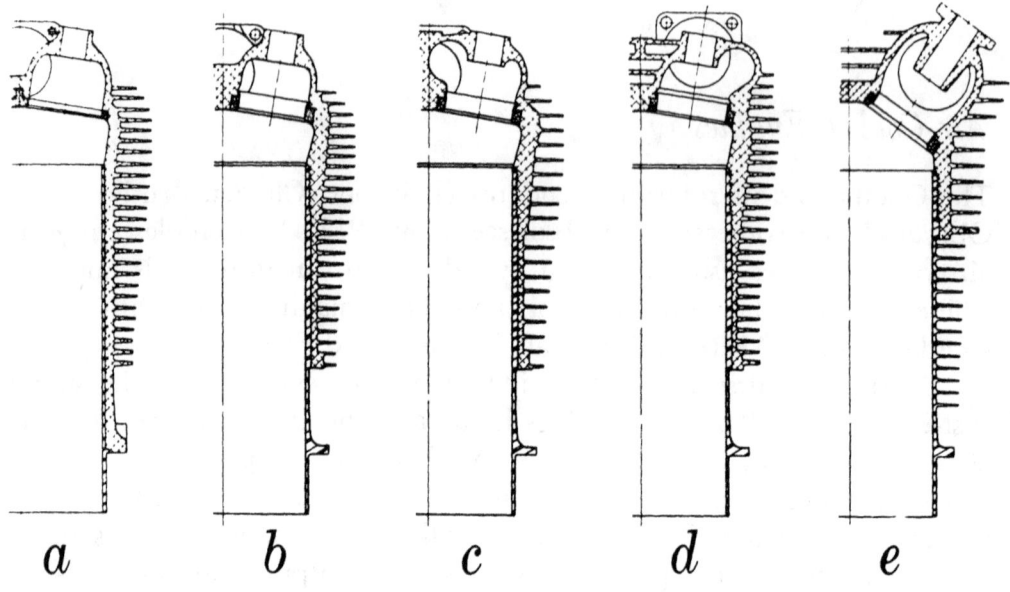

a   b   c   d   e

Figure 36.—Development of air-cooled cylinders in the United States: a, Lawrence J-1 (1922) and Wright Aeronautical J-3 (1923) used cast aluminum structure with thin steel liner. b, Wright J-4 (1924) used flanged steel barrel with screwed-on head and jacket casting. c, Wright J-4A (1924-5) similar to J-4. d, Wright J-4B (1925-6) similar to J-4A but with air passage and fins between the ports. e, Wright J-5 (1926-7) designed by Heron; barrel carries integral steel fins. f, Wright Turbo-Cyclone cylinder of 1948, with forged and machined aluminum head, forged-steel barrel with rolled-on aluminum fins, and sodium-cooled exhaust valves, stellite-faced, has more than 100 square inches of fin area for each square inch of piston area. (a-e, from *Transactions of the Society of Automotive Engineers*, vol. 21, pt. 2, p. 872, 1926; f, courtesy Wright Aeronautical Corporation.)

---

finally a 9-cylinder 200-hp radial in 1921. This was the J-1 (fig. 39), which was supported by an order for 200 engines from the United States Navy. In 1922 Lawrance's company was absorbed by the Wright Aeronautical Corporation [16] and, with Navy support, the 9-cylinder engine was built in improved models known as the Wright J-3, J-4, and J-4b, all with essentially the Lawrance cylinder design (see fig. 36a-d).

During the same period, 1918-1926, S. D. Heron had left England and had been employed by the United States Army Air Service at McCook Field, Dayton, Ohio, to assist in the development of large radial engines.[17] Heron was a devoted worker and an able engineer, and by 1921 had developed successful air-cooled cylinders of nearly 6-in. bore, based on his work with Gibson plus his own improvements worked out at McCook Field.

Against considerable resistance from their chief engineers, who at the time were thoroughly committed to water cooling, the Curtiss Aeroplane Company and Wright Aeronautical accepted contracts from the Army Air Corps to build prototype radial engines with Heron-designed cylinders. Some engines were built, but in very small numbers.

The Lawrance and Heron developments were brought together when Heron in 1926 joined Wright Aeronautical Corporation, of which Lawrance was president. The first result, the Wright J-5, was essentially a Lawrance-type engine with Heron-type cylinders (figs. 36e and 40). This was a successful engine of the 200-hp class, as evidenced by its use in Lindbergh's New York-Paris flight, 20-21 May 1927, in many other pioneering flights, and in a number of early transport airplanes. It won the Robert J. Collier trophy, this country's most sought after aviation award, in 1927. Wright Aeronautical had also been experimenting with air-cooled radial engines

Figure 37.—Bristol Jupiter 9-cylinder engine, 1922; 400 hp at 1650 rpm, 700 lb. This example was built by Cosmos Engineering Co., Ltd. Cylinder design is similar to that of ABC cylinder in figure 35, left. *(Photo A-3104)*

Figure 38.—Armstrong-Siddeley Jaguar 14-cylinder 2-row radial engine, about 1922; 360 hp at 2000 rpm, 910 lb. First successful British radial engine with aluminum-head cylinders and gear-driven supercharger. Cylinder design is similar to that of Gibson cylinder in figure 35, right *(Photo A-3111)*

Figure 39.—Lawrance J-1 air-cooled radial engine, 1922. The first American-designed 9-cylinder radial to be put into general use, its rating was 200 hp at 1800 rpm, 476 lb. The cast-aluminum cylinder head and internally cooled exhaust valves have been retained in modern practice. Cylinder section is shown in figure 36a. *(Photo A-3086)*

Figure 40.—Wright Whirlwind J-5 engine (NASM 121) of 1927; 220 hp at 1800 rpm, 510 lb. This is the type used in transoceanic flights by Lindbergh, Chamberlin, Byrd, and others. Cylinder section is shown in figure 36e. (*Photo A-44092*)

having cylinders larger than those of the J-5, the bore of which was 4.5 in., but the first really successful engine of the larger type was the Pratt and Whitney 425-hp Wasp of 1927.

Subsequent to the merger of Wright and Lawrance, a considerable fraction of the Wright Aeronautical staff, headed by the chief engineer George J. Mead, resigned to join Frederick B. Rentschler in forming the

Pratt & Whitney Aircraft Company of Hartford, Connecticut. In a time almost as short as that for the Liberty engine, this new group produced the Wasp (shown in fig. 41), the first large radial air-cooled engine of what may be called "modern" design. The notable features of this engine included:

- Rating, 425 hp at 1,800 rpm
- 9 cylinders, 5.75x5.75 in. bore and stroke
- Built-in geared centrifugal supercharger
- Fully enclosed valve gear, with rocker boxes integral with cylinder head (fig. 41)
- Forged and machined crankcase (fig. 42)
- Domed-head, 2-valve cylinders, basically of the Heron design
- Divided crankpin (fig. 43) with one-piece master rod

While most of these features had appeared previously, their combination here was an eminently rational and successful one, and set a high standard for future development of radial engines.

The only important basic improvements to be developed later for radial air-cooled engines were:

- The forged and machined aluminum cylinder head, pioneered by Bristol in England and Wright Aeronautical in the United States about 1940 (Gnome had pioneered the forged and machined steel head for air-cooled engines)
- The automatically lubricated (by engine oil) valve gear, pioneered by Pratt & Whitney in 1932 (first used in water-cooled aero engines by Hispano-Suiza, ca. 1914)
- The vibration-absorbing counterweight, introduced by Wright Aeronautical in 1935, which will be discussed later
- Second-order balancing weights, to reduce unbalanced forces

The basic features of the Wasp, with the addition of the above improvements, are used in all modern large air-cooled radial engines. This type, of course, has dominated transport and much of military aviation until the recent advent of the jet and turbine engine. Figures 44-47 show the outstanding modern air-cooled radial engines which are basically descendants of the Gnome, but with greatly improved detail design, including the composite steel and aluminum cylinder construction pioneered by Gibson, Heron, and Lawrance. Figure 36 shows the evolution of Wright cylinders from about 1920 to 1930, in comparison with the cylinder used on the Wright turbo-compound engine, the most highly developed air-cooled radial.

Figure 41.—Pratt & Whitney Wasp air-cooled radial engine, 1926; 425 hp at 1900 rpm, 650 lb. The first such United States engine of over 400 hp to go into general service, it pioneered many technical features which became standard practice for this type. Cylinder design was similar to that of the Wright J-5 (fig. 36e) except that rocker-arm supports and housing were cast integral with the cylinder head—an important innovation. (*Photo A-3087*)

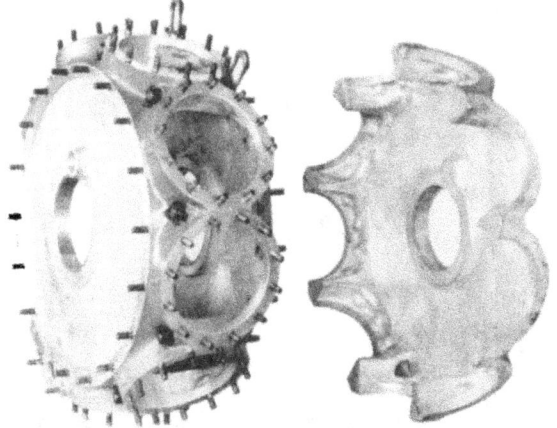

Figure 42.—Forged aluminum crankcase of Pratt & Whitney Wasp engine. Left, complete crankcase. Right, forging of one half before machining. (*Photo A-3105*)

Figure 43.—Divided crankshaft, from Pratt & Whitney Wasp engine. The Gnome (see fig. 20) pioneered this design for radial aircraft engines. (*Photo A-3106*)

Figure 44.—Pratt & Whitney Double Wasp R-2800-CB-16 18-cylinder air-cooled 2-row radial engine, 1946; 2800 hp at 2800 rpm, 2327 lb. Earlier models were extensively used in World War II, and this model was widely used in commercial and military aircraft. (*Photo A-3103*)

Figure 45.—Pratt & Whitney Wasp Major R-4360 28-cylinder 4-row radial engine, 1948 (cutaway); 3500 hp at 2900 rpm, 3842 lb. A post-World War II military and commercial engine. (*Photo A-4132*)

Figure 46.—Wright Cyclone R-1820 1425-hp 9-cylinder engine, 1953. When this engine first came into use in 1933, it was rated at 525 hp at 1900 rpm. It was used in the Douglas DC-3 and Boeing B-17, among others. (*Photo A-3090*)

Figure 47.—Wright Turbo-Cyclone R-3350 18-cylinder 2-row radial engine, 1955 (cutaway); 3700 hp at 2900 rpm, about 3000 lb. This post-war engine had three exhaust-driven turbines geared to the crankshaft, and it was the latest and most highly developed piston type to be widely used in large military and commercial airplanes. (*Photo A-3089*)

The following comparison illustrates the development of air-cooled engines from 1922 to the present time:

Engine	1922 Lawrance J–1	1955 Wright Turbo-Compound
Number of cylinders	9	18
Bore and stroke, in	4.5x5.5	6.125x6.3125
Maximum hp	200	3,700
Rpm	1,800	2,900
Brake mean effective pressure, psi	112	302
Mean piston speed, ft/min	1,650	3,070
Hp per sq in. piston area	1.4	7.0
Weight, lb, per hp, dry (without oil and oil radiators)	2.38	0.96

As had been true of liquid-cooled engines, improvements in fuels, supercharging, and cooling systems as well as great improvements in detail design, were important factors in this development.

The subject of the air-cooled engine should not be left without mention of the remarkable development of the light-airplane engine, beginning with the small British 4-cylinder vertical Cirrus and DeHavilland Gypsy engines of 1927, and of the 4-cylinder Continental A–40 (fig. 48). Introduced in 1931, this 38-hp engine used cast-iron L-head cylinders. It was the forerunner of contemporary horizontal-opposed light-plane engines. Later models use composite aluminum and steel cylinders similar to the J–5 cylinder of figure 36e. Engines of this type built by Continental Motors Corporation and by others, including principally the Lycoming Division of Avco Corporation, have developed to a remarkable degree of reliability and performance. In 1961, a license to build Continental engines of this type was acquired by Rolls-Royce, a real compliment to the high quality of these small powerplants.

Another interesting category of air-cooled engines comprises those built for installation in model airplanes. These are usually 1-cylinder 2-cycle engines of less than 1-in. bore and stroke (fig. 49). Some are rated up to 1 hp at speeds of 15,000 rpm or more. Originating in the United States about 1930, these engines were produced in very large quantities between 1945 and 1950. It is claimed that there were 180 manufacturers of model engines in the United States during that period, and their total production, in number of engines, probably exceeded that of all other aircraft engines combined. The popularity of engine-powered model airplanes fell off about

.—Continental A-40 air-cooled horizontal-cylinder engine, 1931; 40 hp at 2500 rpm, is engine was the forerunner of contemporary opposed light-plane engines. (Photo A-

Figure 49.—Model airplane engine, Super Cyclone (NASM 1944-20), about 1950; about 1/10 hp at 10,000 rpm, 6 ounces. This typical single-cylinder, 2-cycle, air-cooled model engine uses special fuel with hot-wire ignition. (Photo A-36625)

Figure 50.—Frontal coolant radiator for Liberty engine on DeHavilland DH-4 (NASM 1919-51), 1918. This position for the radiator required a large cooling surface and contributed heavily to airplane drag. (*Photo A-9850-D*).

Figure 51.—Completely exposed Lawrance J-1 radial engine on Curtiss F4-C1, about 1924. *Below*, Partially exposed Wright J-5 engine on Ryan NYP airplane *Spirit of St. Louis* (NASM 1928-21), after return from Europe, 1927. (*Photos A-47190, A-1193-B*).

Figure 52.—Radial engine with NACA-type cowling on Frank Hawks' Lockheed Air Express, 1929. (*Photo A-33428-E*)

1950, but has revived during the past decade. During 1966 one manufacturer alone produced a million model aero engines.

Air Versus Liquid Cooling

The classic and often emotionally charged argument over the relative merits of liquid and air cooling started with the early days of flying (Antoinette vs. Gnome, for example) and persisted to the end of World War II, when the advent of jets and turbo props diverted attention elsewhere.

As we have seen, water cooling was dominant through World War I, except for the rotaries, which at its close were obsolescent. European military aviation remained generally committed to water cooling up to and through World War II, although some air-cooled engines were used in bombers and transports, and there was one excellent air-cooled European fighter, the Focke-Wulf with the BMW 2-row radial, developed from a Pratt & Whitney license. Japanese fighter aircraft also used air-cooled radials copied from Wright and Pratt & Whitney designs. Their other military aircraft used these and copies of the German Daimler-Benz liquid-cooled engine (fig. 33).

In the United States, the Navy made a commitment to air cooling in 1921 which has held for reciprocating engines to this day. It was chiefly Navy support that underwrote early Pratt & Whitney and Wright air-cooling developments. The reason for this choice lay in the limitations of the aircraft carrier, which imposed such design criteria as short takeoff, compact size, and minimum maintenance. Commander Bruce Leighton was probably the individual most responsible for this well-considered decision.

The most intense controversy on this subject took place in the United States Army Air Service, whose support for air-cooled engine development in the 1920s and 1930s was never as enthusiastic as that of the Navy, because of the assumed larger frontal area and greater drag of air-cooled radials, especially for use in fighter airplanes. That cooling drag was a real problem in the early days is illustrated by figures 50 and 51, showing typical installations of the 1920s.

The drag of air-cooled engines was greatly reduced by the advent of the very effective cowling and cylinder baffling developed at Langley Field by NACA, starting in 1929 (figs. 52 and 53). Further reductions in cooling drag were achieved by increased cooling-fin area, which reduced the air velocity required for cooling (compare figs. 36a-e and 36f. These develop-

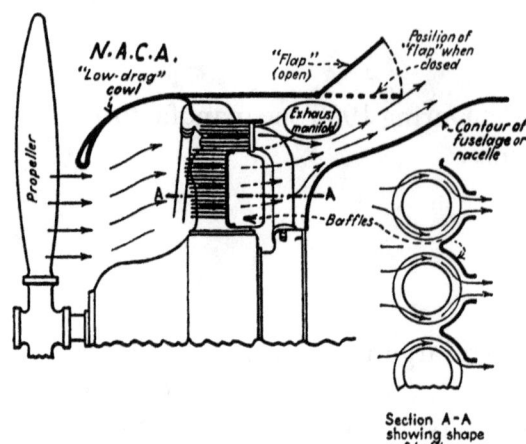

Figure 53.—Cooling-air flow in tractor installation of a cowled radial engine. Only the upper half of the installation is shown.

Figure 54.—Installation of radial engine on a Douglas DC-6, 1949, showing modern cowling for radial engine, with controllable outlet flaps. (*Photo A–50822*)

Figure 55.—Comparison of radiator installations for water (left) and for ethylene glycol cooling, on Curtiss Falcon airplanes, 1930. (From *The Project Engineer*, vol. 13, no. 10, p. 9, 1954, publ. by the Thermix Corp.)

Figure 56.—Liquid-cooled fighter, North American P-51 Mustang of World War II. Coolant radiator is housed under fuselage, below the star insignia. Inlet and outlet ducts are designed to minimize drag. *(Photo A-45801)*

ments put the air-cooled radial virtually on a par with the water-cooled engines with regard to cooling drag, until the advent of high-temperature liquid cooling with glycol-water mixtures. Figure 54 shows modern cowling for the air-cooled radial engines.

The use of high-boiling liquids (mixtures of water and ethylene glycol) for engines formerly water-cooled was an important forward step in reducing the heat-transfer area, and thereby the drag, of radiators for liquid-cooled engines. At the suggestion of S. D. Heron, a 1-cylinder engine was tested at McCook Field in 1923 with a mixture of water and ethylene glycol at a high coolant temperature, probably near 300° F. During 1928–1929 further tests were made at McCook Field with a Curtiss D-12 engine. After considerable development work to avoid leaks and to overcome other troubles encountered, the use of this method of cooling was adopted for Curtiss liquid-cooled engines by 1932, and used soon afterward by Allison and Rolls-Royce. This change, which allowed operation of the coolant at 250° F, reduced the radiator area required by about 50 percent (fig.55). This improvement, together with better radiator design and radiator cowling (fig. 56) brought the drag of liquid-cooled engines well below that of air-cooled radials of equal power. Their installed weight, which had been greater than that of air-cooled radials, also came down to more comparable figures. Schlaifer gives the weight per horsepower of the best liquid-cooled fighter installation in relation to a comparable air-cooled installation as 30 percent more at sea level and about the same at 25,000 ft.[18]

The fact that the Battle of Britain was won by liquid-cooled engines (the Rolls-Royce Merlin) gave a great impetus to the Army prejudice in favor of water-cooled fighters.[19] Actually, both types were used, and it was found that the air-cooled fighter was better at low altitude both because of its lighter specific weight and its lesser vulnerability to small-arms fire.

For commercial uses, however, the elimination of the weight, complication, and maintenance requirements that characterize liquid-cooling has been a chief reason for the popularity of air-cooling for air-transport purposes since about 1932; and with few exceptions, commercial air transports all over the world have used air-cooled engines, mostly of American manufacture, from the early beginnings in the late 1920s up to the present. Although today (1969) jet and turbine engines are standard for large military and commercial airplanes, there are still many more planes powered by air-cooled piston engines, because of their use in planes of smaller size, than by all other types combined.

Unconventional Engines

Hundreds of unconventional types of aircraft engines have been proposed, built, and tested. Among these the following may be mentioned.

BARREL- OR REVOLVER-TYPE ENGINES. In this type the cylinders were positioned around the crankshaft with their axes parallel to it. Its advantage was its compactness, which provided a small frontal area and allowed good streamling. Perhaps the best known was the Almen engine of 1921. None were successful—although during 1929 there were brief demonstrations of the Swiss Statex and British Redrup types, and an example of the latter, the Fury powered a Simmonds Spartan biplane in flight. The methods of linking the pistons to the driveshaft caused lubrication and mechanical problems that were never solved.

FAIRCHILD-CAMINEZ ENGINE. This was a 4-cylinder radial engine (fig. 57) with rollers in the pistons operating on a 2-lobe cam. Its advantages were its small diameter and a propeller shaft running at half engine speed without the usual reduction gearing. The only crankless reciprocating engine to reach the stage of official approval, it received in June 1927 United States Department of Commerce Approved-Type Certificate No. 1. During 1926–28 it was flown experimentally, but it proved impractical because of excessive vibration resulting from torque variation.

SLEEVE-VALVE ENGINES. The earliest development of a sleeve-valve aircraft engine that I recall was that of the Belgian Minerva, a Knight-type, or double-sleeve, engine which appeared in the 1920s, but never got beyond the experimental stage. The single-sleeve, or Burt-McCollum, type, was exploited chiefly in England and finally became operational in the Bristol line of aircraft radial engines, including the Hercules (fig. 58), Perseus, and Centaurus. These were used by the Royal Air Force during World War II. The Napier Sabre, also using the single-sleeve valve, was a 24-cylinder, liquid-cooled, 2-crankshaft H-type engine used in British fighters toward the end of World War II. The Rolls-Royce Eagle (not to be confused with the 12-cylinder Eagle of World War I), a 24-cylinder H-type engine with sleeve valves, was very similar to the Napier Sabre.

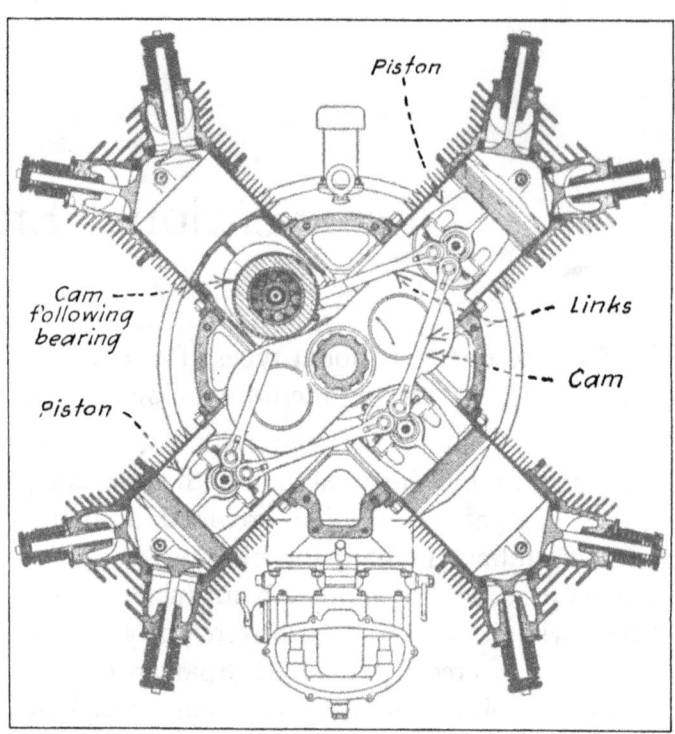

Figure 57.—Fairchild-Caminez engine, transverse section; 135 hp at 1000 rpm, 360 lb. The only crankless reciprocating eingine to reach the stage of official approval, it was later found to be impractical because of severe torque variation. (From Pagé, *Modern Aviation Engines*, 1929, vol. 2, p.1112, fig. 535).

Figure 58.—Bristol Hercules 759 14-cylinder sleeve-valve engine, 1956; 2000 hp at 2800 rpm, 2060 lb. Earlier models were used in British bombers during World War II. (From Wilkinson, *Aircraft Engines of the World*, 1954, p. 244)

It was developed after the war, too late to compete with the rapidly developing jet and turbine engines.

DIESEL AIRCRAFT ENGINES. Diesel engines built by Beardmore and Maybach were used experimentally in some rigid airships during the 1920s. Those used operationally aboard the *Hindenburg* and its little-known sister ship, the *Graf Zeppelin II*, were of Daimler-Benz manufacture. The first diesel engine to power an airplane was a Packard air-cooled radial (fig. 59) designed by L. M. Woolson, who was killed in a crash (due entirely to bad weather) of an airplane powered with one of these engines before the development was completed. The Packard diesel received from the Civil Aeronautics Administration a CAB Approved-Type Certificate 43 on 6 March 1930. It set the world's nonrefueling duration record for heavier-than-air craft 25–28 May 1931, a record that still stands. This

Figure 59.—Packard 4-stroke-cycle 9-cylinder radial air-cooled diesel engine (NASM 1932-7), 1928; 225 hp at 1950 rpm, 510 lb. Although diesel engines had been used earlier in lighter-than-air craft, this was the first to power an airplane. *(Photo A-2388)*

engine and its designer and manufacturer were the recipient of the Robert J. Collier trophy for 1931; however, it never became an important airplane powerplant. The Guiberson air-cooled radial diesel engine appeared about three years after the Packard, receiving a CAB Approved-Type Certificate 79, but was never widely used.

The most successful diesel airplane engine was the Junkers Jumo a 6-cylinder, opposed-piston, water-cooled engine (fig. 60), the development of which was started about 1920. This engine was used to a limited extent in German military airplanes and in German air transport, in the late 1930s. A model fitted with a turbo supercharger powered a high-altitude photographic reconnaissance airplane of World War II, the Junkers Ju-86P, but by that time the engine was obsolescent.

NACA (National Advisory Committee for Aeronautics, later the National Aeronautics and Space Agency, NASA, Washington, D.C.) conducted exhaustive research directed toward the development of aircraft Diesel engines during the decade 1930–1940. This work was centered on injection-system development and combustion-chamber design. No multicylinder engines were built. For reference to this research see *Index of NACA Technical Publications* listed in the first section of the bibliography (p. 96), and also that on diesel engines (p. 112).

The Napier Nomad engine, a 2-cycle diesel compound powerplant was designed after World War II for exceptionally high specific output, but it was made obsolete by the gas turbines before full development.

Numerous other aircraft diesels were built and test flown, mostly in Europe, but by the beginning of World War II, and with the general use of high octane fuels, it became evident that the diesel engine could not compete with the conventional spark-ignition type, and its development terminated. The research work of the NACA on diesel engines for aircraft during the late 1920s and early 1930s was extensive and outstanding, but it found no practical application.

Two-Cycle Gasoline Engines. The earliest 2-cycle aircraft engine flown successfully was built in England by the New Engine Company, Ltd. (NEC), in 1909. It was used in a British-Wright airplane of that period. The cylinders were cross-scavenged with a Roots-type scavenging pump. From 1909 to 1912 both air-cooled and water-cooled NEC engines were built having 2 to 6 cylinders and 20 to 90 horsepower.

A great many 2-cycle gasoline aircraft engines have been proposed, and many were built experimentally. Most of these were of the crankcase-compressor type, now common in outboard marine engines. The attraction of this type of engine lies in its mechanical simplicity and low cost, but it has serious drawbacks for aircraft use, principal among which are its high fuel consumption when used with a carburetor, and its tendency toward misfiring and stalling at light loads. Most of the proposals have been for small, low-cost engines, but so far none has been developed with the characteristics necessary for a truly successful full-scale aircraft engine.

On the other hand, nearly all engines used for model airplanes are 2-cycle and crankcase scavenged, for the sake of mechanical simplicity. In 1966 an engine of this type became available for small target aircraft. The Junkers diesel engine described above stands as the only 2-cycle aircraft engine ever to be used in considerable numbers for military and transport aircraft.

Figure 60.—Junkers Jumo 207-D 2-stroke-cycle 6-cylinder opposed-piston diesel engine (NASM 1966–13); 1200 hp at 3000 rpm, 1430 lb. Photograph shows engine equipped with exhaust-driven turbo-supercharger as used in high-altitude German reconnaissance airplane in World War II. Earlier unsupercharged versions (rated 750 hp at 1800 rpm, 1650 lb) were used in pre-war commercial airplanes. (*Photo A–3112*)

Figure 61.—Napier Lion 12-cylinder W-type liquid-cooled engine, the only W-type ever widely used; 450 hp at 2350 rpm, 985 lb. A racing version, of 800 hp, powered the 1927 winner of the Schneider Trophy, the Supermarine S-5 seaplane, which flew at 281.65 mph. (*Photo A-3098*)

UNCONVENTIONAL CYLINDER ARRANGEMENTS. Finally there should be mentioned some engines with unconventional cylinder arrangements.[20] The first is the Napier Lion (fig. 61), the only W-type engine to see extensive service. This engine was liquid-cooled with its 12 cylinders arranged in 3 rows of 4 each. Brought out in 1918, it was quite widely used in British military and commercial aircraft, and won the Schneider Trophy, a race for seaplanes, in 1927. A second engine in this category is the Pratt & Whitney R-4360, 28-cylinder air-cooled radial with 4 rows of 7 cylinders each (fig. 45). This is the largest (but not the most powerful) successful piston-type aircraft engine ever to reach the service stage. It has been used in many large military aircraft and in the Boeing 377 Stratocruiser. Besides the large number of cylinders and their unusual arrangement in "staggered" radial formation, unusual features include machined-all-over cylinder heads of novel shape and an ingenious arrangement of the pushrod valve gear. This engine would undoubtedly have been more fully developed had it not been for the advent of turbo-jet and turbo-prop engines.

The Rolls-Royce Eagle (the second line with that name) and the Napier Sabre, both using the double-crankshaft H arrangement, have already been mentioned (p. 57).

Related Technical Developments

Fully as important as the historical development of actual engines, has been progress in engine research, leading to improved understanding of the basic phenomena involved. Especial attention under this heading should be given to the improvement in the structural design of aircraft engines made possible by the development of experimental stress analysis;[21] however, a history of research in the field of internal-combustion engines is beyond the scope of this paper. Various sections of the bibliography contain selected references to some of the important contributions in this area. While this list is by no means complete, it should serve as a convenient introduction to the subject. Most of the items listed contain relevant bibliographies.

Interesting related historical developments have also occurred in fuel systems, exhaust systems, control systems, fire extinguisher systems, and many of the other elements comprising the aircraft powerplant. To treat all of these in detail is beyond the scope of this work, but a few are of sufficient importance to deserve mention here.

Valves and Valve Cooling

As previously mentioned, the poppet exhaust valve has always been a critical item because it is subjected to such high gas temperature (up to 3000° F) and high gas velocity, with small areas available (stem and seat only) for heat dissipation to the coolant. One method of attack on this problem has been through the use of improved materials. By 1918 the ordinary steels used at first had given way to high-speed tool steel which has a high degree of strength at elevated temperatures. Tungsten is the chief alloying element in such steel. Unfortunately, this type of steel burns readily at the seat of a leaking valve. Since about 1920 austenitic (high-chromium) steels have been successfully used in various forms, with several other alloying elements, including principally silicon, nickel, and cobalt. A further important improvement, about 1934, was the use of Stellite facing on both valve seats and seat inserts. This development occurred

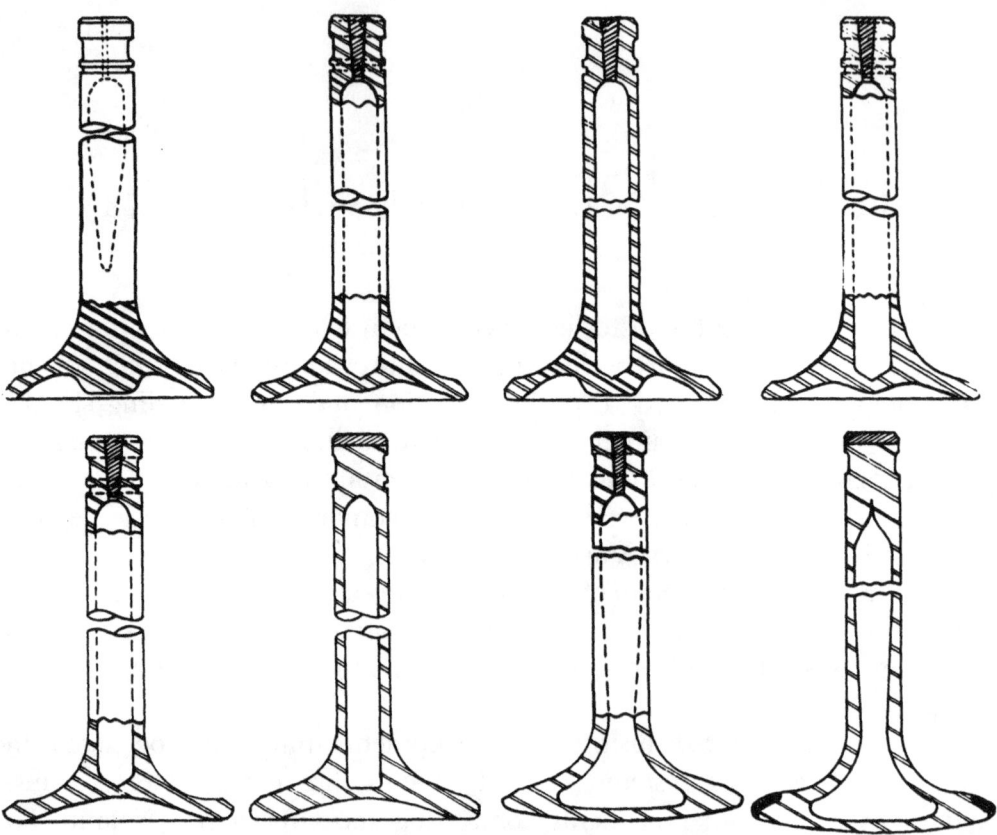

Figure 62.—Evolution of exhaust valves used in Wright radial engines. In all but the first (upper left) the interior space was half filled with sodium to promote heat flow from head to stem and thus to assist in cooling the valve. (From *S.A.E. Journal*, vol. 46, no. 4, p. 150, fig. 9, 1940)

jointly in the United States and abroad (chiefly in Britain), with the manufacturers of poppet valves playing an important part.

Another, and very important, contribution to exhaust-valve life and reliability has been the use of a hollow valve partially filled with liquid for the purpose of improving the conductivity of heat from head to stem. Heron and Gibson tried water in 1913, but the high steam pressure exploded the valve stem. Mercury was next tried, with more success, since its vapor pressure is lower. But mercury will not wet steel. A method of coating the internal valve surface with wettable material was developed by Midgeley and Kettering in 1917, and the Lawrance J-1 9-cylinder radial of 1921 (fig. 39), used mercury-filled valves with some success, although with trouble from mercury leakage.

When S. D. Heron came to McCook Field in 1919, he continued his work on valve coolants and soon used successfully the mixture of sodium and potassium nitrate previously used for heat treating of steel. This material has the necessary low vapor pressure, but its density is low. Continuing his work, Heron by 1928 had adopted liquid sodium as the internal coolant, now used in large aircraft exhaust valves and in many non-aircraft engines.

Figure 62 shows a sequence of development in exhaust-valve design. Much ingenuity has been displayed by valve manufacturers in fabricating the modern hollow-head with hollow-stem valve, and filling it (partially) with metallic sodium.

The automatic lubrication of valves by engine oil, introduced to liquid-cooled engines by Hispano-Suiza (1914) and to air-cooled engines by Pratt & Whitney (1932) has also been an important contribution to the present long life and reliability of aircraft-engine valves.

Another method of attack on the valve-cooling problems was to eliminate the poppet valve in favor of some-form of sliding valve. As already mentioned, the Bristol Aeroplane Company developed its single-sleeve-valve air-cooled radial in the 1930s to the point where it was used in World War II, and the Napier Sabre and the second Rolls-Royce Eagle also had sleeve valves.

Fuels and Combustion

One of the most important developments in aircraft propulsion has been the improvement in, and control of, aviation gasoline. This development is a long and complex story, and only a bare outline can be given here.

For successful use in spark-ignition engines, gasoline must have the proper volatility range, and the highest possible resistance to "knock" or "detonation." Control of volatility seems never to have been a serious problem, and development work in aircraft fuels has centered around increasing their antiknock value. Earliest work on the relation of detonation to fuel composition seems to have been by Harry R. Ricardo in England and by Charles F. Kettering in the United States. Intensive work, under Kettering's direction, was started by Thomas Midgeley and Thomas A. Boyd in Dayton, Ohio, in 1917. During the course of this work it was discovered that some substances, notably iodine, had a strong antiknock effect even in very small concentrations. This discovery led to an intensive search for powerful antiknock agents.

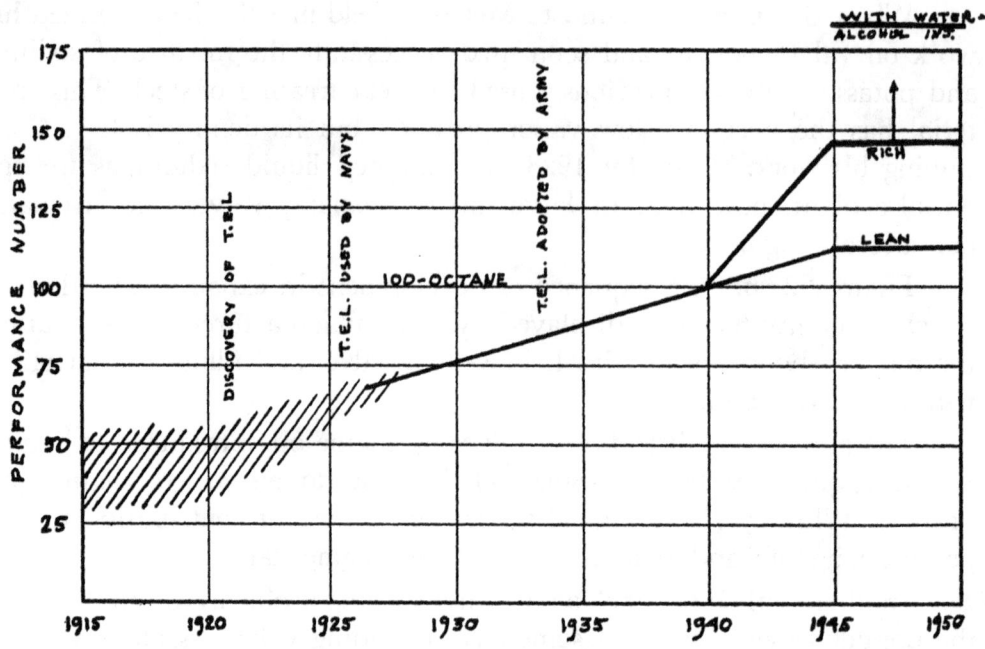

Figure 63.—Increase in aviation fuel performance number with respect to time. The improvement was due both to additions of tetraethyl lead (T.E.L.) and to improved refining methods. Performance number is ratio of knock-limited power to that with pure iso-octane (x100).

Midgeley's work was done on a small 1-cylinder engine in an old Dayton kitchen, and when a promising substance was found there, he would bring it to the McCook Field engine laboratory for test in an aircraft engine. I was closely associated with his work during my administration of that laboratory, 1919–1923. By 1920 toluene and its related compounds appeared promising as an additive and were used in flight tests, notably by Schroeder for the 1920 altitude record with a turbo-supercharged Liberty engine. By 1921 the extreme antiknock effects of metallo-organic compounds was evident, and in 1922 Midgeley brought the first samples of tetraethyl lead, $Pb(C_2H_5)_4$, to McCook Field for tests in 1-cylinder and full-scale aircraft engines. Experimental work with leaded fuel continued thereafter at a rapid pace. It was officially adopted for use in aviation gasoline by the United States Navy in 1926 and by the Army in 1933, and has since become universally accepted as an additive for gasoline.

Another important contribution was Graham Edgar's work, about 1926, in determining the effect of fuel structure on antiknock quality and, specifically, discovering the high antiknock properties of the branched-chain parafins such as iso-octane.

Specifications and laboratory tests for antiknock quality of aviation fuels were sponsored by the Cooperative Fuel Research Committee in 1933, and led to good control of this quality in United States aviation fuels soon after. S. D. Heron was also an important contributor to this result. The "performance number" of a fuel, used from about 1942, is the ratio of knock-limited indicated mean effective pressure (klimep) with that fuel, to the klimep in the same engine using iso-octane.[22] Figure 63 shows the improvement in the performance number achieved both by the use of tetraethyl lead and the control of fuel composition.

The powerful effect of water or water-alcohol injection is also illustrated in figure 63. This development seems to have been started at Pratt & Whitney about 1940, and was continued by them, by the Army Air Corps at Wright Field, and by the NACA laboratories. By 1946, water-alcohol injection was generally used for takeoff by both military and transport airplanes. The high consumption of the auxiliary fluid (about 50 percent of the fuel flow) limits its use to short periods and to engines with sufficient supercharging to take advantage of the increased knock limit.

Altitude Performance and Superchargers

The fact that, as altitude increases, reduced air density reduces engine power must have been realized before it became obvious in 1909, when airplanes began to try for high-altitude flight. The advantage of altitude in military work became very apparent in World War I, but the only attempt at improved altitude performance used in World War I was embodied in the German BMW and Maybach engines, which were designed to be partly throttled near sea level, the throttle to be fully opened only above about 5,000 feet. Both engines were designed to be lighter in weight than would have been required for full-throttle operation at sea level, and the BMW also had higher compression ratios than could be used with full throttle at sea level without detonation. The advantage in altitude performance over an engine capable of full-throttle operation at sea level, however, was quite small.

Measurement of engine performance at altitude was first seriously undertaken when the United States Bureau of Standards completed its altitude test chamber in 1918. Subsequently a considerable literature on this subject developed (see bibliography).

The Swiss engineer A. J. Buchi suggested the turbo-supercharger for aircraft in 1914. This type was then developed in France by Rateau, and experimental models were tested during the war, but none was put into service use. Laboratory work on gear-driven superchargers was conducted during the war by the RAF at Farnborough, England. Intensive development of supercharging equipment began both in England and the United States in 1918.

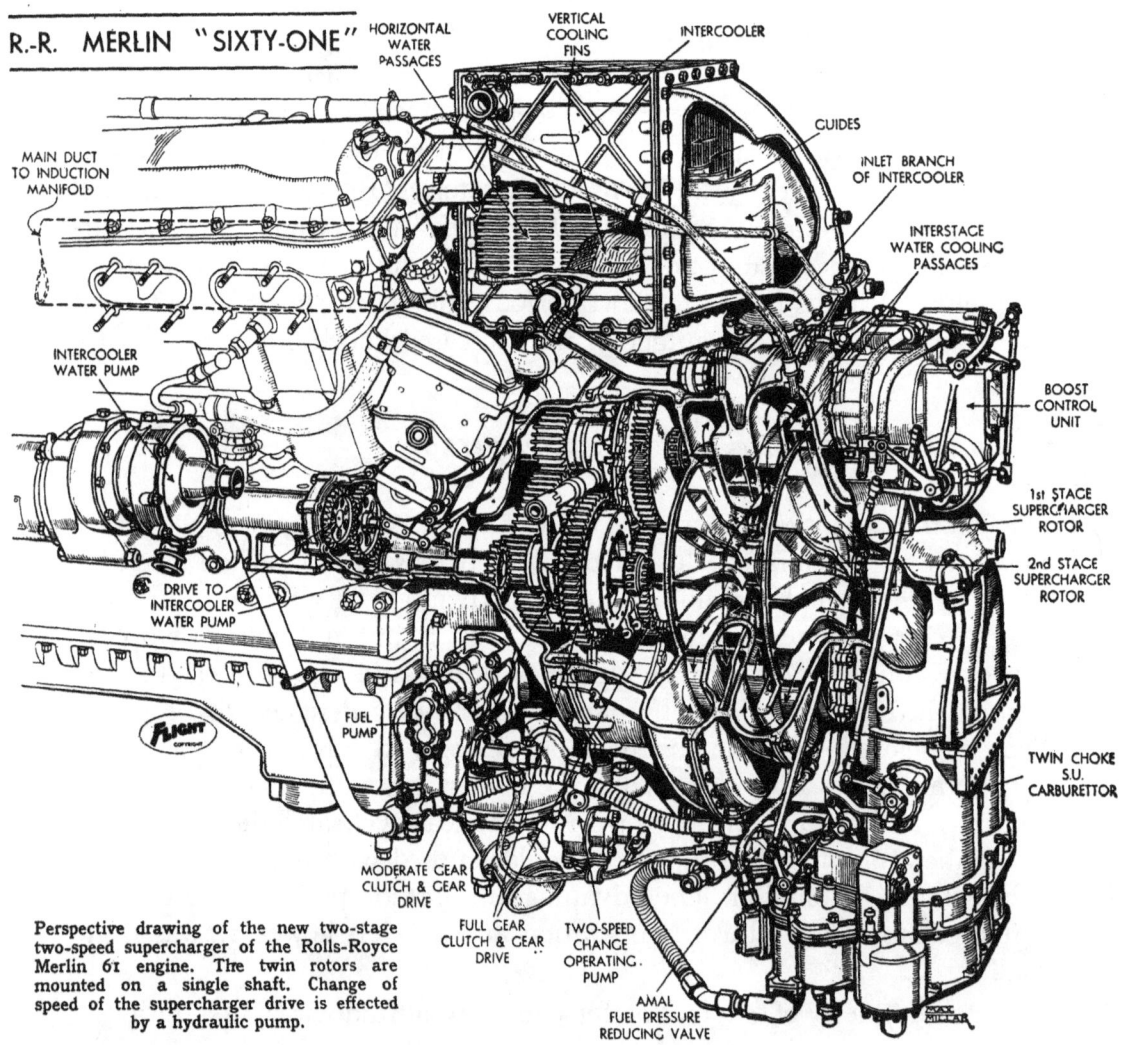

Perspective drawing of the new two-stage two-speed supercharger of the Rolls-Royce Merlin 61 engine. The twin rotors are mounted on a single shaft. Change of speed of the supercharger drive is effected by a hydraulic pump.

Figure 64.—A two-stage two-speed geared supercharger with intercooler and aftercooler, as installed on the Rolls-Royce Merlin 61 engine of 1942, the first of its kind to be used in service. (From *Flight*, vol. 42, p. 656, Dec. 17, 1942)

Many types of compressors have been considered, but only one, the centrifugal type, ever got beyond the experimental stage. The Royal Aircraft Factory had Armstrong-Siddeley construct a radial engine with a built-in geared centrifugal supercharger in 1916, but the design was unsuccessful, probably because of torsional vibration in the drive system. Siddeley did not produce a successful geared supercharger until that used in 1926 in the Jaguar (see fig. 38).

Geared superchargers were built experimentally by Curtiss and by Wright Aeronautical Corporation in 1925, but the first United States production engine to be so equipped was the Pratt & Whitney Wasp of 1927, a year later than the Jaguar. After 1930 all military and transport engines were equipped with geared centrifugal superchargers, and in all cases some kind of flexible coupling was introduced in the gear train to prevent critical torsional vibration. The culmination of the geared centrifugal type is represented by the 2-stage, 2-speed supercharger of the Rolls-Royce Merlin (fig. 64).

In 1918 the Engineering Division of the Army Air Service contracted with the General Electric Company to develop turbo-superchargers of the Rateau type. The man in charge of this development for GE was Dr. Sanford A. Moss, who remained in this position for over twenty years. Experimental models applied to the Liberty engine were tested at the top of Pikes Peak in 1918, and in flight at McCook Field in 1919.

Figure 65 shows an installation of this early type of General Electric supercharger on a Liberty engine. A Le Pere airplane with this equipment held the world's altitude record for the years 1920, 1921, and 1922. Supercharging was hard on an engine not originally designed for it, and I remember when Major Schroeder, who made the 1920 record, returned from a flight with the Liberty engine and its nacelle cut in two by a failed connecting rod at the third crank from the front end. The only elements holding the four forward cylinders and the propeller in place were the crankshaft and the two camshaft housings. In spite of this condition, and the loss of all its cooling water, the Liberty engine was still running!

A serious difficulty with the supercharger shown in figure 65 was the failure of turbine blades due to inadequate cooling of the turbine. In 1922 Ernest T. Jones, in charge of superchargers under Major G. E. A. Hallett, chief of the power plant section at McCook Field, was asked to redesign the General Electric supercharger to overcome this difficulty. In a conference with Jones over the design board, I suggested placement of the turbine wheel on the nacelle surface, using an overhung turbine wheel as in figure 66. This suggestion was adopted for the new design. Turbine

Figure 65.—a, General Electric turbo-supercharger installed on Liberty engine (NASM 1966-43) of the type which held the world's altitude record for 1920, 1921, 1922. Tubes conveying air from compressor to carburetor serve as an aftercooler. b, Night view of turbo-supercharger in operation. The exhaust manifolds and the nozzle box are white hot (about 1500° F) and the turbine, operating at over 20,000 rpm, is surrounded by hot exhaust gas. (*Photo A-3092, A-3193*)

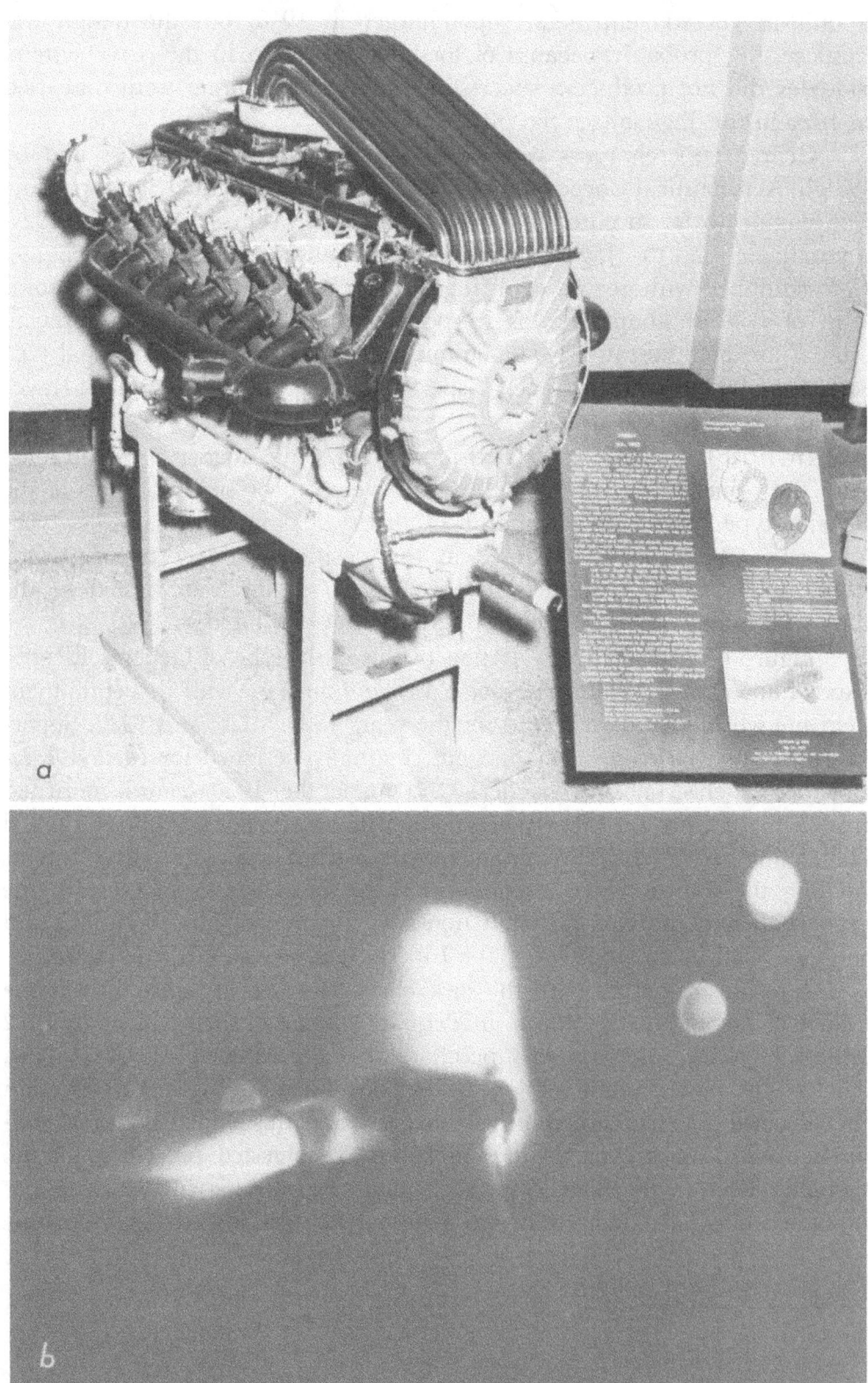

wheels of this type have been used on all subsequent installations of turbo-superchargers in the United States, including the Martin biplane bombers [23] of the 1920s and the B-17 and B-24 bombers and P-38 and P-47 fighters of World War II. The Boeing Stratocruiser and the B-29 and B-50 bombers used essentially the same system, although in these airplanes the turbine was located inside the nacelle and the overhung wheel was cooled by air piped in from outside. Beginning with the B-17 the engines were also equipped with gear-driven superchargers acting as the second stage.

Figure 66.—Side-type turbo-supercharger installed on Curtiss D-12F 460-hp engine in Curtiss P-5 Hawk, 1927. This exposed position of the turbine wheel was effective in reducing the blade temperature as compared to the earlier arrangement shown in figure 65. (Photos A-3094)

Figure 67.—NACA Roots-type supercharger, coupled to Pratt & Whitney Model A Wasp engine, 1927. Bypass valve, lower right, controls inlet pressure. A world's altitude record was established in 1927 with this installation in a Wright Apache airplane. (Photo courtesy Pratt & Whitney)

The only service use of turbo-superchargers on foreign-built airplanes appears to be that of the German Junkers diesel-engine high-altitude photographic plane shown in figure 60. It is remarkable that this very effective device received so little development outside of the United States.

In 1927 the official world's altitude record was taken by Lieutenant C. C. Champion, Jr., USN, with a Pratt & Whitney Wasp equipped with a NACA Roots-type supercharger acting as first stage to the engine's own geared centrifugal equipment (fig. 67). This is the only important use of a noncentrifugal supercharger in aircraft.[24]

Aftercoolers,[25] that is, devices to cool the air after leaving the supercharger, have been generally used with turbo-superchargers, and with 2-stage geared types. Such coolers are shown in figures 64 and 65. The Merlin engine (fig. 64) used a water-cooled aftercooler with its own separate radiator and circulation system.

The culmination of the supercharger art is represented by the Wright Turbo-cyclone R–3350 engine shown in figure 47. This engine, introduced about 1946, has three exhaust-driven turbines geared into the power system, as well as a 2-speed centrifugal geared supercharger. It is standard on the Douglas DC–7 and the Lockheed Super Constellation, the last large piston-engine passenger-transport planes built in the United States.

Vibration Control

Powerplant vibration presents two kinds of problems in aircraft. One is external vibration, or vibration of the power plant with relation to the airplane itself. The other is internal vibration, that is vibration of parts within the powerplant. Considerable external vibration from engine and propeller was accepted as normal in the early days of aviation. In my experience it became of concern first in 1920, with the Hispano-Suiza V–8 300-hp engine, a larger version of the original model. This engine, like all V–8s up to that time, had cranks at 180°, which gave a strong second-order horizontal vibration. It also had an unusually large torque variation, due to its large cylinders and high mean effective pressure. Pilots complained of discomfort with this engine.

About 1921 the Wright Aeronautical Corporation, which produced the 300-hp Hispano engine, built one with counterbalanced cranks at 90°, thus eliminating the horizontal shake. Vibration-measurement at that time was in a crude state, and the improvement obtained was demonstrated on the test stand by the fact that, with the 90° shaft, a penny would remain on the crankcase, whereas with the 180° shaft the penny would quickly bounce off.

The next test was to mount two engines in similar Thomas-Morse fighters, one with the 180° shaft and one with the 90° shaft. A number of engineers ran these engines on the ground, and a number of pilots flew them. The consensus was that there was no noticeable difference in vibration of the airplane. Probably, the engine torque variation was so large in both cases as to obscure the improvement in sidewise shake. In any case, the 90° shaft was not approved, although it soon became standard on V–8 engines for nonaircraft use. Such was the state of vibration analysis in 1922!

Reduction of engine vibration became essential in the early days of commercial aviation when passenger comfort became important. In this case, radial engines were used. Charles S. Draper and George Bentley made a serious study of the shaking forces and movements of radial engines in 1937–1938. One solution lay in flexible engine mounts to reduce the transmission of vibration to the airplane structure. This involved a problem of "droop" due to gravity when the engine was mounted at its rear, as in the case of radials.

There was also the problem of decoupling the several modes of vibration in order to avoid numerous critical speeds. This problem was solved by the mount patented by Edward S. Taylor and K. Browne, which has been widely used since. The principle employed is an arrangement of links which have the effect of supporting the engine at its center of gravity, although the actual flexible mounts are at the rear. Otto C. Koppen has used very flexible decoupled engine mounts in light airplanes with good effect since about 1939. Another contribution to reduction of engine vibration was the adoption by Wright and Pratt & Whitney, in the late 1930s, of second-order rotating weights to balance the second-order shaking component characteristic of the master-rod system in radial engines.

Internal vibration of reciprocating engines has been most serious in the propeller-crankshaft system. This type of vibration originates chiefly from the torque variation inherent in piston engines and may be destructive when resonance is involved. The Liberty engine of 1917 had a torsional resonant speed of 1900 rpm with the usual propeller. Its rating at 1700 rpm was close enough to cause accessory-gear breakage, as previously mentioned (p. 30). Serious trouble with torsional vibration was experienced in the 1920s in dirigible airships using long shafts between engine and propeller. This type of vibration also held back the development of metal propellers, to be discussed later (p. 77).

A very critical case of crankshaft-propeller vibration appeared with the introduction of the geared version of the Wright 9-cylinder 1820-cu-in. radial engine in 1935. This problem was quickly and brilliantly solved by E. S. Taylor and R. Chilton, who developed the pendulous counterweight, which effectively counteracted the principal torque components of the engine and prevented breakages in the drive system. The basic concept was that of E. S. Taylor, for which he received the Reed Award in 1936. Chilton contributed the mechanical embodiment. This type of device has been used in large radial aircraft engines ever since, and also in many non-aircraft powerplants. After the first engines so equipped had been tested, it was found that these inventions had been anticipated in France, but the credit for practical application should go to Taylor and Chilton. It should also be mentioned that the Packard Diesel engine of 1928 (see p. 59) was equipped with spring-loaded pivoted counterweights designed to reduce torsional vibration. These, however, could be effective only at one speed, whereas the Taylor-Chilton design was effective over the entire speed range.

Another important torsional vibration problem was that caused by the gear-driven supercharger rotor. Various types of flexible coupling have been used in the gear train to avoid serious trouble.

Further consideration of vibration problems is included under the heading, Propellers, below.

Propellers

Gibbs-Smith credits the Chinese with first use of the air propeller, on toy helicopters. A helical screw is shown on a DaVinci helicopter drawing of about 1500, and screw propellers were used on dirigible balloons as early as 1784. An early Langley propeller is shown in figure 68a.

The success of the Wright brothers was in no small degree due to the excellent performance of their two counter-rotating airfoil-section propellers, chain driven at 8/23 engine speed, or about 380 rpm. They gave serious attention to propeller design. Apparently they could get no useful data from marine engineers and had to develop their own theory. In doing so, they often argued each other into a reversal of opinion, but finally arrived at a design which Frank W. Caldwell says ran at near optimum ratio of forward speed to tip speed, and had an efficiency of about 0.70.

The Wright propellers were of 3-ply laminated wood, very light in weight. It should, perhaps, have served as a warning to future propeller designers that the first fatal accident—the crash of Orville Wright and Lieutenant Thomas E. Selfridge in 1908, resulting in the death of Selfridge—was caused by a propeller failure. A broken blade set up sufficient vibration to cause the propeller to cut a rudder-bracing wire, upon which the tail came askew and all control was lost.

Wooden propellers were universally used from the time of the Wrights' first flight until well after World War I. They were very reliable for the needs of that time, and were superseded only when the requirements for power and tip speed exceeded the limits within which a wooden propeller would safely operate.

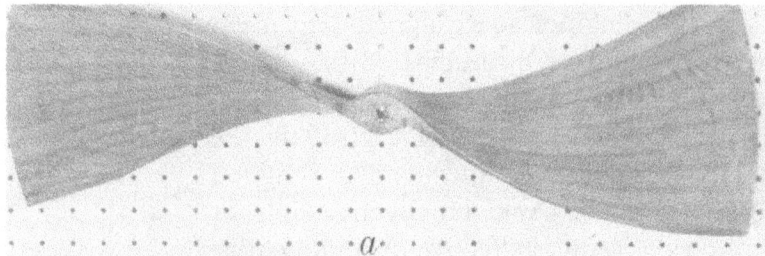

Figure 68.—Propeller development: a, Langley wood propeller (NASM 1938-56E) of 1893, used on Aerodrome No. 4. b, Curtiss-Reed twisted-duraluminum propeller (D-6), 1925. c, Hamilton-Standard 2B20 constant-speed propeller, 1946. d, Hamilton-Standard Hydramatic full-feathering propeller of 1947. For typical wooden propeller of the period 1910 to present, see figure 50. (*Photos, respectively, A-287, A-51875, A-3096, A-3097*)

Materials superior to wood were actively sought after World War I. Frank Caldwell, head of the propeller section at McCook Field (1918–1930) and later chief engineer at Hamilton Standard, was a leader in this field, and has given excellent accounts of propeller developments. Here there is space for only the briefest review.

Micarta (canvas laminated with bakelite) was successfully used as a wood substitute by 1920. In 1921 Caldwell tested a steel-bladed propeller on his electric whirling machine to twice its rated power. He then, very innocently, presented it to me for a "routine" test on a Hispano-Suiza 300-hp engine. After a few minutes at rated power, a blade broke off, came through the control board between the heads of two operators, climbed a wooden staircase, and went through the roof. The engine was reduced to junk.

The above incident was an early warning of the importance of vibration and fatigue in propeller operation. At my insistence, further "routine" propeller tests on experimental propellers were made in a specially constructed "bombproof" shelter. All metal propellers of that time (1921–1922) failed, with murderous results to the engine. In one case the whole assembly of crankshaft, rods, and pistons was pulled out and thrown 20 feet from what remained of the engine and stand.

Subsequent metal propeller development involved careful attention to vibration problems. The Reed type, using a twisted aluminum plate as a base (fig. 68b), was one of the early successful designs. Later, the manufacturers of metal propellers developed elaborate equipment and procedures for the measurement and suppression of blade vibration.

An excellent historical record of the development of variable-pitch propellers is given by K. M. Molson. The idea started with marine propellers as early as 1816. The need for pitch control in airplane propellers was realized as early as 1912. Various designs of controllable-pitch propellers were tested, usually with disastrous results because of mechanical weaknesses. Variable pitch became essential with the advent of the high-performance airplane, the Boeing 247 and the Douglas DC–3 being early examples. Important propeller developments, with approximate dates are:

1921	Aluminum blades, fixed pitch (Reed)
1923	Aluminum blades, adjustable pitch
1931	Hollow steel blades
1929	Controllable pitch, 2-position
1935	Automatic, constant speed
1938	Feathering
1945	Reversible and feathering

The above dates indicate general use in at least some airplanes. Among the first flights with controllable pitch were those at McCook Field with the Heath propeller about 1921. The first application of the constant-speed variable-pitch propeller was by Hele-Shaw and Beacham for a test flight in England in 1928. Both hydraulic and electric pitch control were used until after World War II. Now hydraulic control and aluminum blades are standard on piston engines, with a few exceptions. Figure 68 shows examples.

Reduction Gears

The Wrights, with their chain drive, were evidently aware that the optimum speed for engines is not usually that for propellers. Even before the Wrights, most experimental airplanes (Stringfellow, Maxim, Langley, and others) had belt- or gear-driven propellers, although the drive ratio for steam engines was usually up rather than down.

Direct propeller drive, with the propeller mounted on the crankshaft, is attractive for its simplicity and reliability, and was used by most of the early fliers after The Wright's and up to the start of World War I. An exception was the early Renault air-cooled V-8 (fig. 17, p. 20), the propeller shaft of which was an extension of the camshaft (or vice-versa) and ran at half crankshaft speed—a ratio which has been widely used since.

Other geared engines which appeared for use in World War I included the RAF (a copy of the Renault), the 8-cylinder-in-line Mercedes, and the 220-hp Hispano-Suiza. These were soon followed by the Rolls-Royce Eagle, with planetary gears.

The need for propeller gearing results from the fact that the propeller speed for optimum propeller efficiency is usually lower than the speed at which the engine gives its best performance. Without gearing, the speed for the engine-propeller combination is chosen as a compromise—too high for best propeller efficiency and too low for maximum engine power. As improved engine design called for higher engine speeds, this compromise became more unsatisfactory. By 1920 most large European engines were geared. In the United States, however, the general use of reduction gears came much later. For that matter, in 1924 gearing was actually eliminated from the Curtiss D-12 engine in order to save 25 pounds of weight! Nevertheless, by 1930 it was evident that large engines should be geared to allow of optimum performance. Pratt & Whitney used an internal gear in 1931, and both Wright Aeronautical and Pratt & Whitney adopted the Farman planetary gear for use in the DC-3 in 1933 (fig. 69). From that time on,

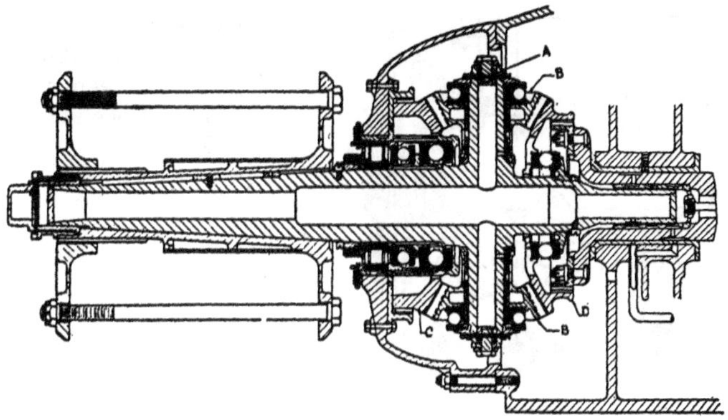

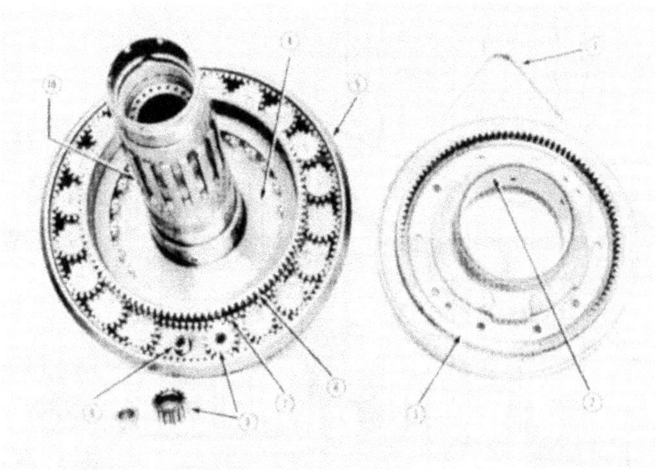

Figure 69.—Bevel planetary reduction gear system as used on Farman engines, after World War I. This type was also used by some American engine builders under license from Farman. *Below,* Spur-type planetary reduction gear system which superseded the bevel type.

propeller reduction gears became an integral part of all large airplane engines, spur type planetary gears being standard for most radials and plain 2-element spur gears for V-type engines (fig. 70). The plain spur gears used by the Rolls-Royce Merlin of 1945 carried 2,200 takeoff horsepower satisfactorily on a face 2-in. wide, a remarkable achievement in gear design.

Other Developments

Only brief mention can be made here of the numerous secondary, though often very important, problems encountered and solved in the development of reciprocating aircraft engines. Among these, however, should be mentioned the following:

IGNITION SYSTEMS. As mentioned previously, the Wright Brothers' engine of 1903 used "make-and-break" ignition. This system involved a pair of contacts within the cylinder, one insulated and connected to a battery

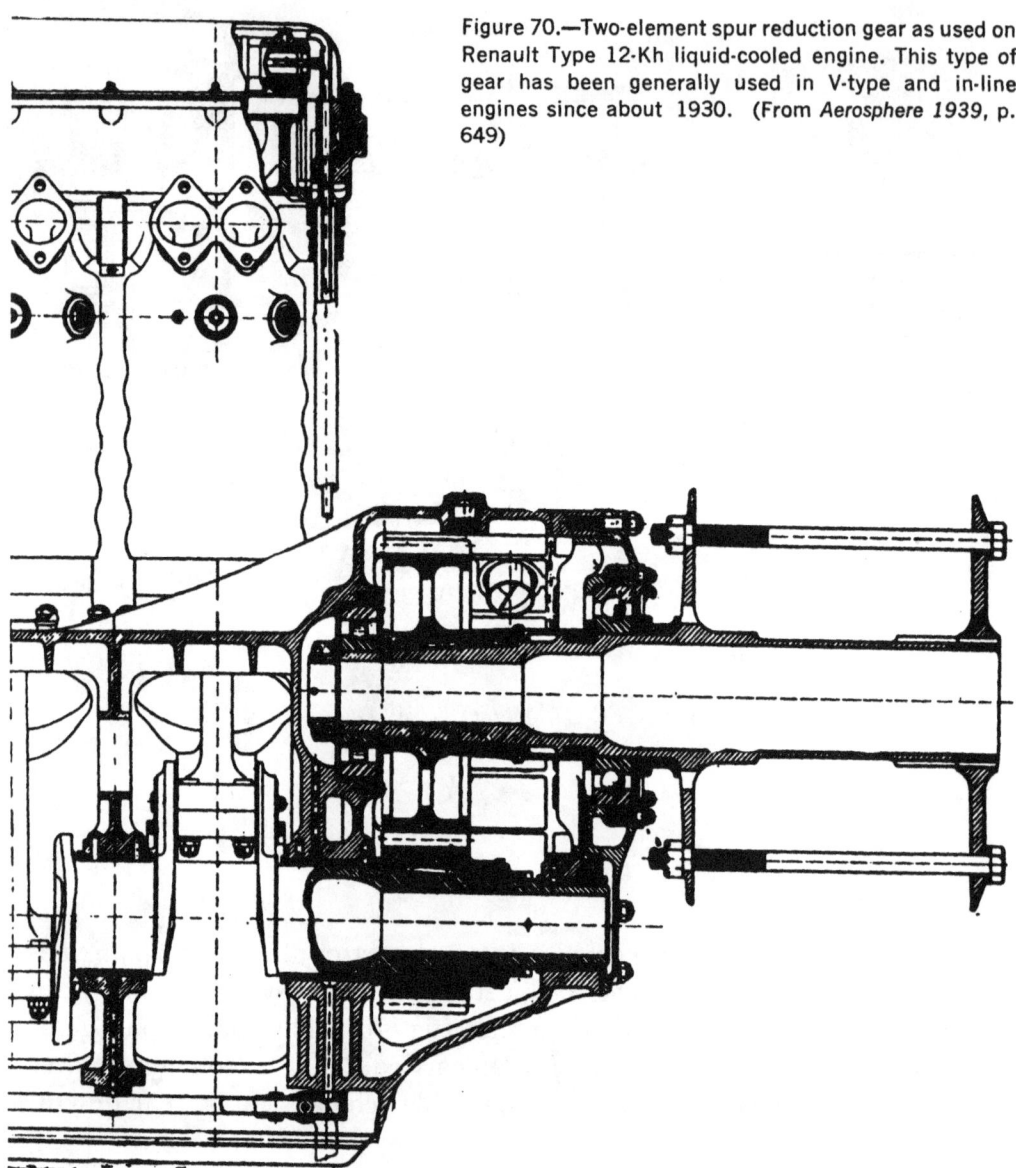

Figure 70.—Two-element spur reduction gear as used on Renault Type 12-Kh liquid-cooled engine. This type of gear has been generally used in V-type and in-line engines since about 1930. (From *Aerosphere 1939*, p. 649)

and coil system and one operated by a shaft protruding through the cylinder wall. This shaft was operated from the camshaft so as to "break" the contact points apart at the moment of ignition. The low voltage arc so formed was an effective igniter. However, the mechanical complication involved, and the difficulty of cooling the contact levers within the cylinder made it impractical for any but very low-output engines. This system was soon displaced by the "high-tension" system with spark plugs which was used in all other successful airplane engines, and, in its essentials, is accepted practice to date for all spark-ignition engines.

Ceramic-insulated spark plugs were generally used in the United States before 1921. Both mica and ceramic plugs were used in Europe. From about 1921 to 1940 mica plugs were generally used. The development of new ceramic materials about 1940 caused a universal change to this material.

CARBURETION. At the time of the Wright brothers' first flight, little was known about carburetion, and various devices were used to introduce fuel to air. As mentioned earlier (p. 13), the Wright brothers used gravity fuel feed from a small can to a heated surface in the inlet pipe. Manly used a large sheet-metal box filled with porous wooden blocks, a scheme originally conceived by Balzer. These blocks were saturated with fuel, and the engine air was drawn past them, in the hope that a combustible mixture would result. The Antoinette engine and all of the Wright brothers' engines produced during 1907–1912 used a small pump to inject fuel into the inlet ports. The carburetion system used for the Gnome rotary engine has already been described (p. 25). All these systems required experimental adjustment, good for only one engine speed.

Meanwhile, float-type carburetors were being developed for automobile use, and these were used by most aircraft engines after the Gnome and Antoinette. Float-type carburetors were used by the Wright brothers on their later engines, and were generally used for aircraft engines up to about 1935. A floatless carburetor was introduced by the Chandler-Groves Corporation in 1935, and the Stromberg floatless injection-type carburetor became operational about 1938. Since that time most military and transport engines have used floatless-type carburetors, many of the injection type. Light-plane engines have, generally, continued to use float-type carburetors, although injection systems are available for this type.

FUEL INJECTION. Direct injection into the individual cylinders was used in gasoline engines for a short time on some Pratt & Whitney Wasps in 1931–1932. This method was developed to service use in World War II in German military engines. It was adopted by Wright Aeronautical Corporation for their R–3350 engine in 1944.

Injection through nozzles located at each inlet port, first used on the Antoinette engine of 1906, has been used to a limited extent in light-aircraft engines since about 1946.

STARTING. Hand starting by the propeller was standard before 1920. Subsequent development included simple hand cranks, hand cranks with inertia flywheel, cartridge starters, air starters, and finally the present electric starter with storage battery.

BEARINGS AND LUBRICATION. Most radial engines, even as early as the Gnome (fig. 20), used ball or roller bearings for the crankshaft. This practice has been continued with few exceptions, of which figures 44 and 45 show examples. Ball or roller bearings occasionally have been used for crankpins (see figs. 20 and 33). Thrust bearings generally have been of the ball type.

Most aircraft engines have used plain journal bearings for the crankpin, and, with the exceptions noted above, for the main crankshaft bearings. Before about 1930 such bearings were made of the lead-tin-antimony alloy babbit. This material is excellent for bearings in all respects except in structural strength, which is low.

After about 1930 the increases in power and speed, resulting in increased bearing loads, began to cause serious fatigue failure of plain babbit bearings. Meanwhile a subsidiary of the General Motors Corporation had developed a bearing material consisting of a copper matrix filled in with lead. These "copper-lead" bearings were found to have excellent load carrying ability as compared to babbit, and were soon adopted as standard for all high-output aircraft engines.

During World War II, U.S. radial engines started to have crankpin-bearing failures when overspeeded in combat dives. A bearing consisting of a steel shell lined with a thin layer of cadmium, with a very thin overlay of silver was developed to solve this problem. Variations on this bearing have been used in large radial-engines crankpins since that time. Copper-lead bearings, when improved with a very thin overlay of tin, have generally been found adequate for V-type engine crankshafts and crankpins.

These bearing developments have been an important factor in the up-rating of airplane engines illustrated by figure 71.

Improvements in lubrication systems have included the use of full pressure feed to bearings, rather than gravity or splash feed, or such "total loss" systems as that already described for the Gnome engine (see p. 23). Another important improvement has been the installation of adequate oil filtering elements within the engine's oil-circulation system. As size and power of engines has increased, it has become necessary to limit oil temperature by circulating the lubricant through oil radiators, usually air cooled.

The use of castor oil as a lubricant for most, if not all, aircraft, engines previous to 1918, has already been mentioned (p. 25). When fresh, this type of oil is an excellent lubricant, but has the disadvantages of rapid breakdown to gummy deposits in the engine, and a very limited supply base. Work to explore the possibilities of petroleum oils for aircraft-engine lubrication was started at the United States Navy Aero-Engine Laboratory at Washington, D.C., in 1917, and within a few months a number of proprietary mineral oils were found satisfactory and approved for use in all except rotary engines. Since that time, development of mineral oils suitable for aircraft engines has been energetically carried on by the oil industry. The resulting improved quality of lubricants has been an important factor in increasing the reliability, and the running time between overhauls, of aircraft piston engines.

ENGINE INSTRUMENTS. The development of engine instruments has been concurrent with that of the engines themselves. The earliest flights were made without any engine instruments at all. Early instruments were chiefly for the purpose of indicating whether or not the engine was performing satisfactorily (in fact this is still the purpose of most engine instruments carried in aircraft). First to come into use was some sort of tachometer for observing engine speed. It was followed, in the approximate order of use, by sight glasses or gauges to indicate oil flow or oil pressure, remote-reading temperature gauges for oil and coolant, and thermocouples for indicating the temperature of air-cooled cylinders at some critical point. As flight duration increased, fuel-supply indicators, usually showing fuel-level in tanks, were found important. The introduction of supercharging required manifold-pressure indicators. A late development in engine instruments is the engine "analyzer," an electronic system which observes the ignition-voltage versus time curve of any cylinder on a cathode-ray screen and which requires the services of a flight engineer. Used in most large multi-engine airplanes, it enables a trained observer to detect and anticipate many forms of engine trouble or incipient failure by observing these curves for each cylinder in turn.

A detailed account of instrument history and technology is beyond the scope of this volume. Chatfield, Taylor, and Ober in the various editions of *The Airplane and its Engine* (1928–1948) give descriptions of instruments as they appeared at the time of publication. Other relevant publications will be found in the bibliography.

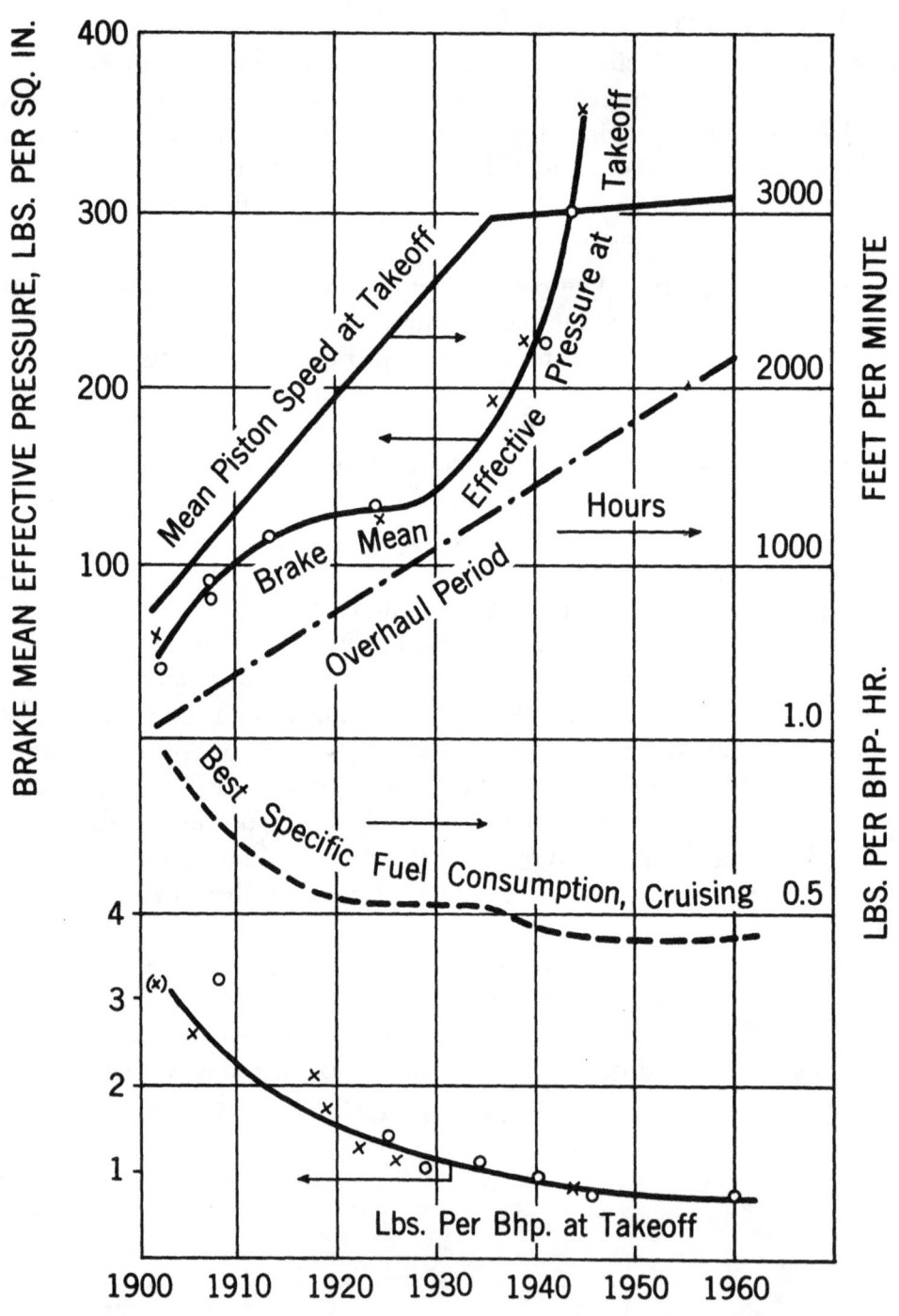

Figure 71.—Engine development curves. Typical performance characteristics of military and large commercial airplane piston engines, 1903–1960. From 1930 on these curves apply to supercharged engines; unsupercharged engines, except as regards overhaul period, remain at approximately the 1930 levels.

Summary of Piston-Engine Development

Figure 71 shows performance parameters for piston aircraft engines since 1903.

Brake mean effective pressure (bmep) is a measure of an engines' ability to withstand high cylinder pressures and to produce power with a given speed and size. Starting at 62 psi (Langley, 1902), it rose to 130 by 1925, which is near maximum for unsupercharged engines. With the introduction of supercharging and improved fuels in the 1930s, bmep was increased to takeoff values up to 360 psi (Rolls-Royce Merlin) and 300 psi (large radial engines in the United States), where it has remained since the advent of jets and turbines.

Mean piston speed (mps) at takeoff rose steadily from 750 ft/min in 1903 to a maximum of 3,000 ft/min in 1935, where it has remained.

Specific fuel consumption has been reduced from nearly 1 lb/hp-hr to current minimum values of less than 0.40. This improvement has been achieved partly through improved design and partly because improved fuels have allowed higher compression ratios (from about 4.0 in 1903 to present values, up to 8.0.

Best weight per horsepower in 1903 was that of the Manly engine, at 2.6 lb/hp. This figure was reduced to 1 in 1935 and has gone slightly below that since (see table 1).

One of the most remarkable improvements has been in reliability and reduced maintenance. The very early aircraft engines were overhauled after every flight. The approved overhaul period for the best modern transport piston engines is now as high as 2,600 hours.

Further improvements in piston engines would have been made had it not been for the introduction of turboprop and turbojet engines, which virtually put an end to intensive development of the large piston engine. Jet engines are also used for certain categories of small aircraft.

Figure 72 shows the piston-engine family as it has developed, finally culminating in the V–12 liquid-cooled engines as represented by the Rolls-Royce and Packard Merlin, and the 18-cylinder air-cooled radials, by the Pratt & Whitney R–2800 and the Wright 3350, of which the

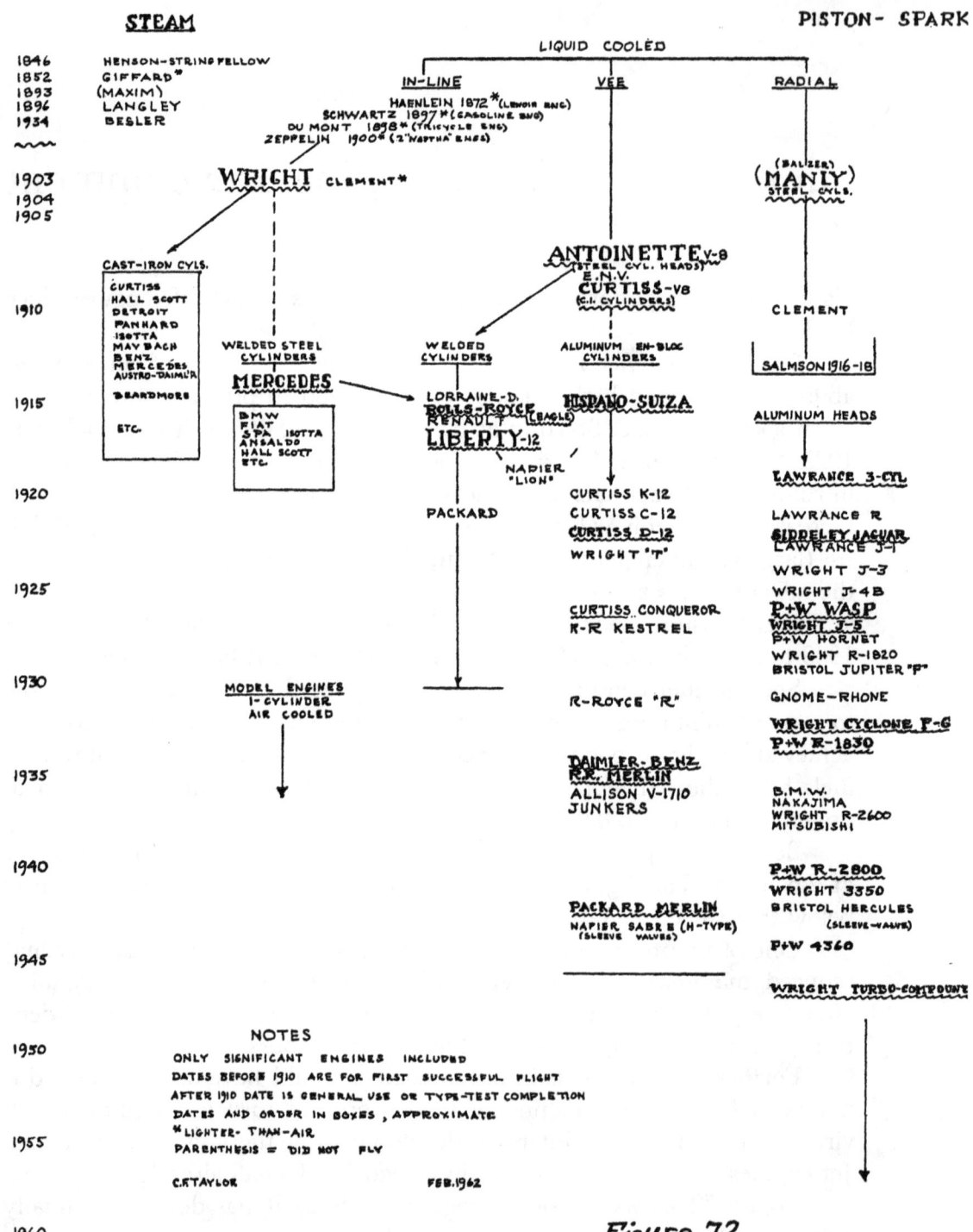

Figure 72

Family Tree
IGNITION

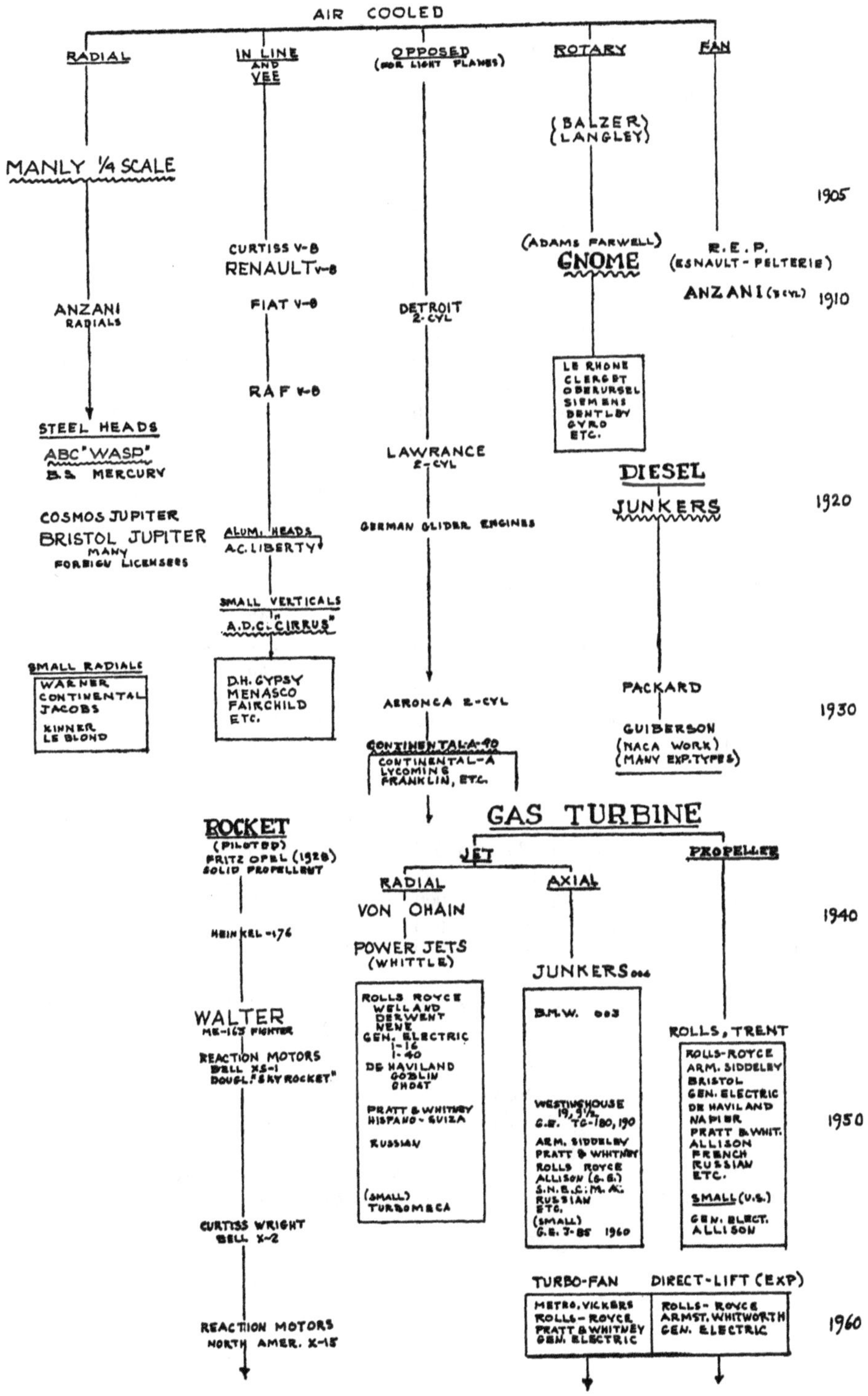

TABLE 1.—Engines of Historical Importance

Engine	Year [a]	Type	No. cyl.	Bore (in.)	Stroke (in.)	Displ. (cu. in.)	Horse-power [b]	Rpm	Weight [c] lb	Weight [c] lb/hp	Bmep (psi)	Piston speed (ft/min)
Water-cooled												
Langley	1901	radial	5	5	5.5	687	52	950	135	2.6	63	870
Wright	1903	horizontal	4	4	4	200	[d] 16	1,090	179	11.2	58	725
Antoinette	1906	V	8	3.15	3.15	196	32	1,400	93	2.9	91	735
Darracq	1909	opposed	2	5.2	4.72	194	24	1,500	121	5.04	65	1,180
Curtiss OX-5	1910	V	4	4	5	503	90	1,400	320	3.55	101	1,170
Mercedes	1915	vertical	6	5.51	6.3	901	160	1,400	618	3.86	100	1,470
Hispano-Suiza	1915	V	8	4.72	5.11	718	150	1,450	467	3.1	114	1,235
Liberty	1917	V	12	5	7	1,650	420	1,700	856	2.04	118	1,985
Curtiss D-12	1922	V	12	4.5	6	1,145	325	1,800	704	2.16	125	1,800
Rolls Royce Kestrel VI.	1930	V	12	5	5.5	1,296	560	2,500	992	1.77	137	2,290
Rolls Royce Merlin I	1936	V	12	5.4	6	1,650	1,030	3,000	1,320	1.28	165	3,000
Packard-Merlin	1945	V	12	5.4	6	1,650	2,250	3,000	1,740	.78	360	3,000
Air-cooled												
Langley (model)	1901	radial	5	2.06	2.75	46.5	3.2	1,800	7	2.2	30	825
Anzani	1909	fan	3	4.13	5.12	206	24.5	1,600	145	5.9	59	1,360
Renault	1908	V	8	2.76	4.72	226	35	1,400	242	6.9	88	1,100
Gnome	1909	rotary	7	3.93	3.93	335	50	1,150	165	3.3	103	753
Jupiter	1920	radial	9	5.75	7.5	1,753	400	1,650	700	1.75	109	2,060
Jaguar	1922	2-row-radial	14	5	5.5	1,512	360	2,000	910	2.53	94	1,830
Lawrance J-1	1922	radial	9	4.5	5.5	787	200	1,800	476	2.38	112	1,650
Pratt & Whitney Wasp.	1926	radial	9	5.75	5.75	1,344	425	1,900	650	1.53	132	1,820
Wright 1820	1930	radial	9	6.13	6.88	1,823	575	1,900	940	1.64	......	2,180
Wright 1820	1945	radial	9	6.13	6.88	1,823	1,525	2,750	1,376	.90	245	3,150
Continental A-65	1938	opposed	4	3.88	3.63	171	65	2,350	155	2.38	128	1,420
Pratt & Whitney 2800.	1940	2-row-radial	18	5.75	6.0	2,804	2,000	2,700	2,300	1.15	209	2,700
Pratt & Whitney 2800.	1945	2-row-radial	18	5.75	6.0	2,804	2,800	2,800	2,327	.83	305	2,800
Pratt & Whitney 4360.	1948	4-row-radial	28	5.75	6.0	4,363	3,500	2,700	3,470	.99	235	2,700
Wright 3350	1941	2-row-radial	18	6.13	6.31	3,347	2,000	2,400	2,848	1.43	197	2,550
Wright 3350	1955	2-row-radial	18	6.13	6.31	3,347	3,700	2,900	3,560	.96	302	3,070

[a] Refers to year of first general use (except for Langley engine). Where two dates are given, they refer to typical early and late models of the same basic engine.

[b] Maximum rated, or takeoff power.

[c] Radiator, cowling, and coolant are not included in the weight of liquid-cooled engines Cowling is not included for air-cooled engines.

[d] Dropped to 12 hp after 1 min.

All liquid-cooled engines later than Curtiss D-12 are supercharged.

All air-cooled engines later than Lawrence J-1, except Continental, are supercharged.

latter two remain in air-transport service, as do also the Pratt & Whitney R–1830 and Wright R–1820 (in the DC–3 airplane). There are also some Pratt & Whitney 9-cylinder Wasp and Wasp Jr. engines in service in medium-powered airplanes, especially in Canada, and a few remain in service in the old Ford trimotors dating from about 1930. A few Pratt & Whitney R–4360 28-cylinder engines also remain in service.

Where the piston engine continues to reign supreme is with the popular light plane. Literally tens of thousands of air-cooled, horizontally opposed piston engines manufactured by Continental, Lycoming, and Franklin power American light planes; and they have their counterparts in lesser quantities in Europe. Although by no means as dramatic as the powerplants that count their horsepower in four digits, these modest prime movers have enjoyed greater quantity production than any other type of aero engine except those for model airplanes.

Figure 72 also includes a family tree for rocket, turbo-jet, and turboprop engines. The history of these developments is so recent and so well covered in the literature (particularly by Schlaifer and Gibbs-Smith) that no attempt will be made to cover it here. There could well be a paper as long as this one, or even a whole volume, devoted to this important and revolutionary development in aircraft propulsion.

It is interesting to review the contributions of the various nations in the field of aircraft propulsion. Table 2 summarizes this subject. It is evident that the United States and France have been the principal contributors to early engine development, while England has made significant contributions in late piston and early turbine engines, and Germany was the first to fly rocket and jet engines, although German and British turbojet development was concurrent.

If the art and science of aircraft propulsion develop as fast in the next 50 years as they have since the Wright brothers' initial flight, the following prophecy of Lester D. Gardner in *Aviation* (vol 1, no. 1, August 1916), will be as meaningful today as it was then:

> Now many of the most distinguished scientists in all countries are giving aeronautics close and careful study. From the work of these men aeronautics will derive the information upon which progress, such as has never been thought possible, will be achieved.

TABLE 2.—Credits, by Country, for Engine Developments

First manned flight	Engine	Aircraft	Year
AUSTRIA			
Internal combustion engine	Lenoir gas engine	Haenlein (dirigible)	1872
DENMARK			
Fixed radial engine air-cooled	Ellehammer	Ellehammer	1906
ENGLAND			
With gear-driven centrifugal supercharger	Armstrong Siddeley	Armstrong Siddeley	1917
Transatlantic nonstop	Rolls-Royce Eagle	Vickers Vimy	1919
Automatic constant-speed propeller	Bristol Jupiter	Gloster Grebe	1928
Turbo-propeller engine	Rolls-Royce Trent	Meteor	1945
FRANCE			
Steam engine	Steam	Giffard (dirigible)	1852
Electric motor	Electric motor	Tissandier (dirigible)	1883
Air-cooled Otto-cycle engine	Tricycle engine	Santos-Dumont (dirigible)	1898
Helicopter	Antoinette V-8	Cornu helicopter	1907
Rotary radial engine	Seguin Gnome	Voisin	1909
More than 8 cylinders	Levavasseur Antoinette 16-cylinder	Antoinette	1910
Propeller reduction gear	Renault V-8	Farman	1910
Inlet-port fuel injection	Antoinette	Antoinette	1906
Seaplane (floats)	Gnome	Heurig Fabre	1910
Turbosupercharger	Rateau	R.A.F. 4D	1918
GERMANY			
Rocket engine	von Opel	Opel–Sander Rak–1	1929
Diesel engine in commercial transport	Junkers 2-cycle opposed piston	Junkers G–38	ca. 1936
Jet engine	von Ohain	Heinkel He–178	1939
Axial flow jet engine	Junkers Ju–004	Messerschmitt 262	1944
Rocket engine in military service	Walter	Messerschmitt 163	1944
SPAIN-SWITZERLAND			
Aluminum cylinder structure	Hispano-Suiza	Spad 7	1914

United States

First manned flight	Engine	Aircraft	Year
Airplane	Wright	Wright	1903
Seaplane (flying boat)	Curtiss	Curtiss	1912
Over 400 hp	Liberty	DeHavilland-4	1918
Transatlantic with 2 stops	4 Liberties	Navy-Curtiss NC-4	1919
With fuel antiknock	Liberty	DH-4 (McCook Field)	1921
Metal propeller	Reed	Standard J-1	1921
Controllable-pitch propeller	Hispano-Suiza	Curtiss JN-4 (McCook Field)	ca. 1921
Over 200 mph	Curtiss D-12	Curtiss racer (Detroit)	1922
Crankless engine	Caminez	Fairchild	1926
Roots supercharger*	Liberty	DH-4 (NACA)	1927
Diesel engine	Packard	Stinson Detroiter Monoplane	1928
Cylinder fuel injection with spark ignition	Pratt and Whitney	Ford or Fokker	1931
With pendulum-type vibration absorber	Wright 1820	Wright Experimental	1935

*As stated (p. 60), the British two-cycle NEC engine used a Roots-type scavenger blower, but this was not a supercharger in the sense that it was used for altitude compensation

Footnotes

[1] The plane had a wing span of 80 ft, a wing area of 300 sq ft, a fuselage length of 25 ft, and weighed 130 lb. The pilot was required to develop 0.4 hp. in order to fly the plane, which had a cruising speed of 21 and a stalling speed of 16 mph. Details of its tests are contained in the catalog of the Shuttleworth Collection, the British museum where it is exhibited. (See "Southampton University Man Powered Aircraft (1960)" In *The Shuttleworth Collection of Historic Aeroplanes,* ... Described by Wing Commander T. E. Guttery, ... Old Warden Aerodrome, Biggleswade, Bedfordshire, 1969, pp. 70–71. In May of the following year, according to the Christian Science Monitor (May 18, 1962, p. 21), the Puffin, a specially built monoplane of 84-ft span, weighing 115 lb, with the propeller behind the tail, was flown under pedal power a distance of half a mile by John Wimpenny at St. Albans, also in England.

[2] These models, Aerodromes 5 and 6, are in the Smithsonian's National Air and Space Museum (NASM 1905-1 and 1905-2).

[3] Without water or flywheels, but with ignition battery. This condition is the same as for the weights quoted for other liquid-cooled engines.

[4] Later development shows this to have been unnecessary. Steel cylinder bores have been used since the Gnome engines of 1909.

[5] Also in 1907 Curtiss broke the World's motorcycle speed record (137 mph) with a 40-hp V-8 air-cooled engine.

[6] See Appendix A for a description of the unique working of the rotary engine.

[7] The Navy version was a slight modification having dual ignition and a 100-hp rating.

[8] The details of this feat are related in *Smithsonian Annals of Flight*, vol. 1, no. 3, "The Liberty Engine, 1918–1942," by Philip S. Dickey III, Lt. Col. USAF, Ret.

[9] The Wasp, however, did not go into real quantity production nearly as quickly as did the Liberty.

[10] The first nonstop Atlantic crossing was by Alcock and Brown, about a month later, 14–15 June 1919, using two Rolls-Royce Eagle engines (see fig. 25), also with welded-cylinder construction.

[11] The story of this flight is related in *Smithsonian Annals of Flight*, vol. 1, no. 1, "The First Nonstop Coast-to-Coast Flight and the Historic T–2 Airplane," by Louis S. Casey.

[12] It will be recalled that the Wright brothers also used crude aluminum en bloc water-jacket construction on their first engine. Subsequent engines, however, had separate cylinders.

[13] The K was for Charles B. Kirkham, who conceived the basic design for this series and was also consulted in the design of the earlier Liberty engine (see p. 30).

[14] Named for the brother of General William (Billy) Mitchell.

[15] The chief limitations on the cast-iron cylinder are poor heat conductivity as compared with aluminum, and low strength as compared with steel.

[16] See previous remarks, page 33, regarding the Hispano-Suiza engine.

[17] The author was in charge of the engine laboratory at McCook Field, and was closely associated with Heron and his work during this period.

[18] Owing to the fact that radiator area can be designed large enough for any altitude, while fin area on an air-cooled cylinder has a practical limit; the power of air-cooled engines above a certain altitude is therefore limited by cooling.

[19] On one occasion I asked a high-ranking officer: "Does the Army want liquid-cooled fighters even if better fighters can be built around air-cooled engines?" He answered in the affirmative!

[20] Obviously, the sleeve-valve Napier Sabre and the Junkers Diesel also had unconventional cylinder arrangements.

[21] An important contribution to this art in the United States was the development of Stresscoat by E. S. Taylor and Greer Ellis in 1938. This method of showing stress patterns by means of a brittle lacquer coating had been used by the Germans earlier, but was not used in this country until the work of the above-mentioned persons. Experimental stress analysis, using strain gages and photoelastic techniques as well as Stresscoat, has been generally used in aircraft-engine development since about 1940.

[22] For official definitions of fuel terms, including performance number, see fuel handbooks published by the American Society for Testing Materials, Philadelphia, Pennsylvania.

[23] A squadron of Martin bombers was the first combat group ever equipped with turbo-superchargers (1923–1924).

[24] The NEC 2-cycle engines of 1909–1912 were equipped with Roots-type scavenging blowers, but these were not superchargers in the sense that they were used for altitude compensation.

[25] When the cooler is used between stages of supercharging, it is called an intercooler, when it is used between the supercharger and the engine, it is called an aftercooler.

Appendix
The Rotary Radial Engine

The radial engine has been built in two essentially different configurations: the static radial, which still enjoys widespread use; and the rotary (rotating) radial, which passed out of use soon after 1918. The former may be considered a "conventional" engine, in which the pistons, reciprocate inside the cylinders of an engine firmly attached to the airframe.

In the rotary radial, however, the anti-propeller end of the crankshaft is attached to the airframe, and the cylinders and crankcase, to which of necessity the propeller is fixed, rotate around the crankshaft (see figs. 20 and 21). The rotary engine functions internally in exactly the same manner as the conventional radial engine, but because of this arrangement the pistons do not reciprocate relative to the mounting structure, and therefore no unbalanced forces result. Thus, in operation, the rotary engine is exceptionally free from vibration. As mentioned in the text (p. 25), the large flywheel effect of the rotating cylinders was important in relation to the type of control system used at the time.

The rotary radial engine shares with the conventional radial the advantages of compactness, short crankshaft, and adaptability to air cooling. On the other hand it has the following inherent disadvantages:

1. Severe limitations on rpm, resulting from high centrifugal forces created within the revolving engine and wind drag caused by the rotating cylinders.
2. Design limitations imposed by the rotation of all parts except the crankshaft.
3. An undesirable gyroscopic effect on the airplane during turns.
4. Limitations on the lubrication system, which, owing to the design of the engine, resulted in high oil consumption and the throwing out of excess oil with the exhaust, as mentioned in the text.
5. Difficulty of providing a closed exhaust system.

In spite of these disadvantages, however, the rotary engine was an excellent design for the state of the art during the two decades after 1900. It was produced in large quantities during 1914–1918, and powered many successful fighter planes.

Bibliography

Expanded and Arranged by Dr. Richard K. Smith
From Material Furnished by C. Fayette Taylor

This bibliography is limited to material, mostly in the English language, which the author considers important in connection with the history of aircraft propulsion, and with which he is familiar. An exhaustive bibliography including all important foreign references would be a desirable project for some future historian.

The first section of the bibliography contains books and periodical articles in which the emphasis is on the historical aspects of engine development. The second and third sections, comprised mainly of references to topical articles in the periodical literature, is arranged chronologically by date of publication. This was done on the assumption that anyone using this bibliography is more likely to be familiar with the time period in which a development has occurred that with an author's name.

NACA (National Advisory Committee for Aeronautics—later the National Aeronautics and Space Administration, NASA, Washington, D.C.) carried out, and also sponsored, exhaustive and important research in airplane engine technology. For a complete list of its publications in this field, see the index of NACA publications, listed in the first section of this bibliography. Especially relevant NACA reports are included on pages 123 to 134, and are referenced under the appropriate headings.

Bibliographies and Indexes

BROCKET, PAUL, ed. *Bibliography of aeronautics of the National Advisory Committee for Aeronautics* [now NASA]. Washington, D.C.: U.S. Government Printing Office. Published during the years 1910 through 1932, when further work on it was unfortunately abandoned, this valuable source had its inception when the editor was assistant librarian at the Smithsonian Institution, and the first volume appeared as volume 35 of the *Smithsonian Miscellaneous Collections*.

GAMBLE, WILLIAM BURT, ed. *History of aeronautics. A selected list of references to material in the New York Public Library, 1938.* New York Public Library publication, 1938. 325 pp. Originally published as a series in the New York Public Library *Bulletin* (January 1936 to September 1937). See especially "Engines," 122–128.

National Advisory Committee for Aeronautics. *Index of NACA technical publications, 1915–1949.* 1950. 605 pp. See also bibliography of NACA Reports, p. 123.

History and Technology of Aircraft and Flight

Certain aspects of the history of aircraft propulsion are also treated in publications listed under Aircraft Powerplants: *Aircraft Power Before 1900* (VILLENEUVE, 1868–1869). *Engines 1900–1913* ("Airship After Buyer," 1903; "The Failure of Langley's Aerodrome," 1903; SANTOS-DUMONT, 1904; "Samuel Pierpont Langley," 1906; "The White Flyer," 1906; "The Wright Aeroplane . . . ," 1906; HOWLAND, 1908; "Types of Recent Foreign Flying Machines," 1908; WRIGHT, 1908; "The Aero Exhibition," 1909; "The Paris Aviation Exhibition," 1909). *Engines 1914–1919* (DOUGLAS, 1919). *Engines 1920–1924* (BAUMAN, 1920). *Engines 1925–1929* (LEIGHTON, 1929).

Certain aspects of theory and technological practice are also treated in publications listed under Aircraft Powerplants: *Engines 1914–1919* (DURAND, 1918; UPTON, 1918). *Engines 1920–1924* (LOENING, 1920; SPARROW, 1921). *Engines 1925–1929* (MCCORD, 1925; CLEMENTS, 1928; FOKKER, 1928; BROOKS, 1929). *Engines 1930–1934* (LYON, 1930; DIETRICH and LEHR, 1932; TAYLOR, 1933). *Engines 1935–1939* (LOMBARD, 1937; KAMPER, 1939). *Engines 1940 and After* (DEFOREST and ELLIS, 1940). Also under NACA Reports: *1st, 1915* (LUCKE); *2d, 1916* ("Nomenclature for Aeronautics"); *4th, 1918* (TICE); *6th, 1920* (DICKINSON and NEWELL); *10th, 1924* (SPARROW); *12th, 1926* (WARE); *13th, 1927* (GARDINER and SCHEY); *17th, 1931* (MARVIN and BEST); *24th, 1938* (GERRISH and VOSS).

ABBOT, C. G. The 1914 tests of the Langley Aerodrome. *Journal of the Aeronautical Sciences,* vol. 10, no. 1 (January 1943), pp. 31–35, drgs., footnote refs.

ANGLE, GLENN D., ed. *Airplane engine encyclopedia; an alphabetically arranged compilation of all available data on the world's airplane engines.* Dayton, Ohio: Otterbein Press, 1921. Illustrations and data on successful and unsuccessful engines to 1920; includes several fine fold-out drawings.

———., ed. *Aerosphere; including modern aircraft, modern aircraft engines, and aircraft statistics and buyer's guide.* New York: Aircraft Publications, annually, 1939–1943. An encyclopedic work of *Jane's* format. The engine section was sometimes published as a separate volume, *Aerosphere's modern aircraft engines.*

The aviation industry. *Lubrication,* vol. 38, no. 4 (April 1952), pp. 37–52, illus., historical tab. data, bibl. of 9 items.

BANE, THURMAN H. Recent advances in aviation. *SAE Transactions,* vol. 15, pt. 2, 1920, pp. 63–86, illus. Bane was chief of the U.S. Army Air Service's Engineering Division at McCook Field, Ohio.

BANKS, F. R. The aviation engine. *Proceedings of the Institute of Mechanical Engineers,* vol. 162 (1950), pp. 433–445. General article on progress and development in engines and accessories, 1920–1950.

BONNEY, WALTER T. *The heritage of Kitty Hawk.* New York: W. W. Norton, 1962. 211 pp., illus.

CHATFIELD, CHARLES HUGH, and TAYLOR, CHARLES FAYETTE. *The airplane and its engine.* New York: McGraw-Hill Book Co., editions 1928, 1932, 1936, 1940, and 1949. Textbook discussions of the subject; each edition outlines the status of airplane propulsion as of its respective date.

DAVY, M. J. B., and RICHARDS, G. TILGHMAN. *Aeronautics; A handbook of the collections illustrating aeronautics;* Volume 3, *The propulsion of aircraft.* London: His Majesty's Stationery Office, 1930. 104 pp., illus. Divided into historical and technical surveys, and a catalog of exhibits as of 1930. Includes 2 pp. of bibl.

DICKEY, PHILIP S. The Liberty engine, 1918–1942. *Smithsonian Annals of Flight*, vol. 1, no. 3, 1968, 110 pp. Generously illustrated; graph and tab. data.

DRIGGS, IVAN H., and LANCASTER, OTIS E. *Gas turbines for aircraft.* New York: Ronald Press, 1955. 349 pp., illus., drgs., diagrs. Chapter 11 is devoted to the history of this type.

DRYDEN, HUGH. Our heritage from Wilbur and Orville Wright. *Journal of the Aeronautical Sciences*, vol. 30, no. 12 (December 1953), pp. 803–804.

Ellehammer: A Danish pioneer who first flew 50 years ago. *Esso Air World*, vol. 8, no. 4 (July–August 1966), pp. 16–19, illus. Although his "flights," 1906–1908, were inconsequential short hops, Ellenhammer's engine was unusual in its low wt/hp ratio at this early date.

FAUROTE, FAY L., Airplane types. *SAE Transactions*, 1918 pt. 2, pp. 137–202, illus. Airplanes up to 1918, including history starting with Wright brothers.

FROESCH, CHARLES. A review of commercial air transport from its beginning—its future and problems. *SAE Transactions*, vol. 71, 1963, pp. 272–280, 292, illus. Brief article, useful in recognizing engines used and their approximate dates of introduction to commercial flying.

GEISSE, J. H. Twenty-five years of engine design. *Aviation*, vol. 25, no. 23 (December 1, 1928), pp. 1720–1723, illus. Special issue, 25th anniversary of flight at Kitty Hawk; also includes, pp. 1727–1765, a very useful series of brief histories of aeronautical manufacturers.

GIBBS-SMITH, CHARLES H. *The aeroplane; an historical survey of its origins and development.* London: Her Majesty's Stationry Office, 1960. 375 pp., illus. with 22 pp. photos. A scholarly and well documented history of heavier-than-air flight that includes 10 pp. of chronology, a 5 p. glossary, and 4 pp. of bibliography. This book is perhaps the most authentic and well-documented work available in its field, and includes much valuable material on power plants.

———. *The invention of the aeroplane, 1799–1909.* New York: Taplinger Publishing Co., Inc., 1966. 360 pp., illus. with photos, drawings, and sketches. Complete and authentic, with emphasis on technical details rather than historical events. Lists all engines flown, 1903–1909.

GODDARD, ESTHER C., and PENDRAY, GEORGE EDWARD, eds. *Rocket development; liquid fuel rocket research, 1929–1941.* New York: Prentice-Hall, Inc., 1961. 222 pp. History of the pioneer work of Robert H. Goddard in rocket development, as edited from Goddard's notes and memoranda.

HARPER, HARRY. "The first air display: A veteran aviation journalist recalls the Rheims meeting 40 years ago. *Flight*, vol. 56, no. 2121 (August 18, 1949), pp. 188–190, illus. Account of first European air meet, Rheims, 1909; speed contest won by Curtiss at 47 mph.

HAYWARD, CHARLES B. *Practical aviation; an understandable presentation of interesting and essential facts in aeronautical science.* Chicago: American Technical Society, 1919. 784 pp., illus., drgs., diagrs. An 88-p. section treats engines; glossary of 15 pp.

HERON, SAMUEL D. *History of the aircraft piston engine; a brief outline.* Detroit: Ethyl Corporation, 1961. 130 pp. Chiefly history in U.S., including engines and fuels by an engineer actively engaged in aircraft engine development since 1915.

HOBBS, LEONARD S. The aircraft engine. *The Bee Hive*, vol. 24, no. 4 (fall 1954), pp. 3–10, illus. Author was chief engineer of Pratt and Whitney.

HODGSON, J. E. *The History of aeronautics in Great Britain from earliest times to the latter half of the 19th century.* Oxford University Press, 1924. 436 pp., illus., drgs. The appendices, pp. 373–418, include a chronology and an excellent annotated bibl. keyed to the text's chapters. The text includes good accounts of work of Stringfellow and Henson.

HOLZER, HEINRICH. *Die Berechnung der Drehschwingungen und ihre Anwendung im Maschinenbau.* Berlin: Julius Springer & Co., 1921. 199 pp., illus., diagrs. Reprinted by Edwards Brothers, Inc., Ann Arbor, Mich., in 1948. A classic work on engine vibration.

HOURWICH, ISKANDER, and FOSTER, W. J. *Air Service engine handbook.* Dayton, Ohio: Engineering Division, McCook Field, U.S. Air Service, 1925. 738 pp., illus., diagrs., drgs., extensive graph and tab. data. Exhaustive data on engines of that period.

HUNSAKER, JEROME C. Aeronautics. *Journal of the Franklin Institute*, vol. 253, no. 1 (January 1951), pp. 48–57. Historical survey of its technological aspects.

———. *Aeronautics at the mid-century.* Hew Haven: Yale University Press. 1952. 116 pp., illus.

———. Forty years of aeronautical research. *Annual Report . . . of the Smithsonian Institution . . . for the year ended June 30, 1955*, pp. 241–271, 1956.

Jane's all the world's aircraft. Published annually since 1909, except 1915 and 1921; its editors and publishers vary over the years.

KELLY, FRED C. *The Wright brothers; a biography authorized by Orville Wright.* New York: Harcourt Brace and Co., 1943. 340 pp.

———, ed. *Miracle at Kitty Hawk; the letters of Wilbur and Orville Wright.* New York: Farrar, Straus, and Young, 1951. 482 pp., illus.

LAHM, FRANK P. The Wright brothers as I knew them. *Sperryscope*, vol. 8, no. 10 (April 1939), 1–5, illus.

LANGLEY, SAMUEL PIERPONT, and MANLY, CHARLES M. Langley memoir on mechanical flight. *Smithsonian Contributions to Knowledge*, vol. 27, no. 3, 1911, pp. 1–309, generously illus., with photos, drgs., and diagrs. Ch. 3 and 4 of pt. 1 treat with early engines; pt/2, by Manly describes the full-scale radial engine and the attempts at flight.

LAWRANCE, CHARLES L. Air cooled engine development. *SAE Transactions*, vol. 17, pt. 1, 1922, pp. 431–477, illus., drgs., graph data. The United States pioneer of the air-cooled radial engine.

LEY, WILLY. *Rockets, missiles and space travel.* New York: Viking Press, 1961. 436 pp., illus., drgs., diagrs., tab. data. Includes some historical material on rocket engines; has 18 pp. of very useful bibl.

Lindbergh's Wright Whirlwind a result of seven years' development; work begun on Feb. 28, 1920, and since that time seven successive models of air-cooled engines have been produced. *Aviation*, vol. 22, no. 25 (June 20, 1927), pp. 1358–1359, 1396, illus., drgs.

LOENING, GROVER. Fifty years of flying progress. *Journal of the Franklin Institute*, vol. 256, no. 6 (December 1953), pp. 493–521, illus. Author was noted airplane designer 1918–1940.

LOUGHEED, VICTOR. *Vehicles of the air: A popular exposition of modern aeronautics with working drawings.* Chicago: The Reilly & Britton Co., 1909. 514 pp., illus., drgs., diagrs., tab. data. Work of Penaud, Ader, Wright, Santos-Dumont, Voisin, Maxim, Langley, *et al.* Well illustrated. The author, who subsequently changed his name to "Lockheed" was one of the brothers who founded the Lockheed Aircraft Co.

MAGOUN, FREDERICK ALEXANDER, and HODGINS, ERIC. *A history of aircraft.* New York: Whittlesey House, McGraw-Hill Book Co., 1931. 495 pp., illus. Includes a 5-p. bibl., and 25 pp. of chronology; text is documented throughout. An excellent survey to its date of publication.

――――, and ――――. *Sky high: The story of aviation.* Boston: Little, Brown and Co., 1935. 414 pp., illus. A somewhat more popularized edition of their *A history of aircraft* (1931).

MARKS, LIONEL S. *The airplane engine.* New York: McGraw-Hill Book Co., 1922. 454 pp., illus., drgs., diagrs. A textbook with technical data on engines up to 1921.

MCFARLAND, MARVIN C., ed. *The papers of Wilbur and Orville Wright.* 2 vols. New York: McGraw-Hill Book Co., 1953. Letters of the Wright Brothers, including many of their own drgs., diagrs., etc.

MCMAHON, JOHN ROBERT. *The Wright brothers, fathers of flight.* Boston: Little, Brown and Co., 1930. 308 pp., illus.

MCSURELY, ALEXANDER. The horsepower at Kitty Hawk. *The Bee Hive*, vol. 28, no. 1 (January 1953), pp. 7–11, illus.

MEAD, GEORGE J. The development of fixed, radial air-cooled engines. *SAE Transactions*, vol. 24, 1929, pp. 418–422, illus. Emphasis is historical.

――――. Historical development of air-cooled engines. *Aero Digest*, vol. 14 (February 1929), pp. 42–44, 224, 226–228.

――――. Some aspects of aircraft engine development. *SAE Transactions*, vol. 20, pt. 2, 1925, pp. 809–851, illus. This article covers development of the improved Hispano-Suiza engines, and of the large liquid-cooled V-12s and Lawrance-type radials developed by Wright Aeronautical Corporation. It was written just before Mead left Wright to become one of the founders of Pratt and Whitney and its first chief engineer.

MEYER, ROBERT B., Jr. Three famous early aero engines. *Annual Report of the . . . Smithsonian Institution for the Year Ended June 30, 1961*, pp. 357–372, illus., 1962. Good descriptions of the first Wright brothers' engine, the Langley-Manly-Balzer radial. and the Clement engine used briefly by Santos-Dumont.

On a great pioneer. *The Aeroplane*, vol. 22, no. 13 (March 29, 1922), pp. 221–222. Obituary on Levavasseur, designer of the Antoinette airplane and engine.

PRATT, P. W. Aircraft propulsion systems in evolution. *Astronautics and Aeronautics*, vol. 3, no. 3 (March 1965), pp. 60–66.

REBER, SAMUEL, LT. COL., USA. Recent progress in military aeronautics. *Journal of the Franklin Institute*, vol. 180, no. 4 (October 1915), pp. 437–448.

RICARDO, SIR HARRY RALPH. *Engines of high output; thermodynamic considerations.* London: Macdonald and Evans, 1926. 110 pp., illus., diagrs.

———. The development and progress of the aero engine. *Journal of the Royal Aeronautical Society* (December 1930), vol. 34, pp. 1000–1015, graph data.

SCHLAIFER, ROBERT, and HERON, S.D. *Development of aircraft engines and aviation fuels; two studies of relations between government and business.* Boston: Harvard University Press, 1950. 754 pp. Text documented. Pp. 1–544 by Schlaifer, on engines; 547–662 by Heron, on fuels; 665–705, technical appendices.

Search of archives reveals interesting engine histories. *The Bee Hive*, vol. 12, no. 4 (April 1938), pp. 2–5. Pratt & Whitney development history.

SMITH, G. GEOFFREY. *Gas turbines and jet propulsion for aircraft.* London: Flight Publishing Co., 1942. 79 pp., illus., drgs., diagrs. An unusually fine survey, and at this early date it is strong on historical development.

SQUIER, GEORGE O., MAJOR, USA. The present status of military aeronautics. ASME, *Transactions*, vol. 30, 1908, paper 1210, pp. 639–721, illus. An excellent survey.

———, BRIG. GEN., USA. Aeronautics in the United States. *SAE Journal*, vol. 5, no. 6 (December 1919), pp. 402–414. An excellent survey.

TAYLOR, C. FAYETTE. History of the aeronautical engine; basic features almost unchanged through development years. *Aviation*; vol. 21 (August 16, 1926), pp. 284–286, illus.

TRUE, WEBSTER P. Operation Homecoming. *Sperryscope*, vol. 11, no. 8 (winter 1949), pp. 1–2, illus. Return of the Wright airplane from England to the U.S.

The two R's—A commemorative history of Rolls-Royce aero engines. *Flight*, vol. 65, no. 2363 (May 7, 1954), pp. 571–583, illus. An outstanding survey.

VEAL, C. B. Manly, the engineer. *SAE Transactions*, vol. 34, 1939, pp. 145–153, illus. Historical, with footnote documentation.

VINCENT, J. G. The trend of aviation development. *SAE Transactions*, vol. 17, pt. 1, 1922, pp. 881–898. Vincent was a principal designer of the Liberty engine and was chief engineer of the Packard Motor Car Company.

WILKINSON, PAUL H. *Aircraft diesels.* New York: Pittman Publishing Corp., 1940. 275 pp. Illus., drgs., diagrs., extensive tab. data. Short history and description of some 15 different makes.

———. *Aircraft engines of the world.* New York: Paul H. Wilkinson, an annual publication, 1944–1959. Average of 280 pp. per vol. A combination encyclopedia and catalog of current types.

WALCOTT, CHARLES D. Samuel Pierpont Langley and modern aviation. *Proceedings of the American Philosophical Society*, vol. 65, no. 2, 1926, pp. 79–82. Account of flight of reconstructed airdrome with arguments for the machine as the "first one capable of sustained free flight carrying a man."

Aircraft Powerplants

Classification in this section is by date of publication. Many entries contain data on earlier engines. For articles dealing with unconventional engines, see also under *Engines 1925–1929* (DENHAM, 1926; "The Fairchild-Caminez Engine," 1926; "Cam Engine Passes Fifty Hour Test," 1927; "The Continental Single Sleeve Valve Engine," 1927; "Performance of Fairchild Airplane Engine Improved," 1927). *Engines 1930–1934* (HALL, 1930). *Engines 1935–1939* ("Perseus Production," 1938; "The First Sleeve Valve Engine in Production," 1938). *Engines 1940 and After* (HERRMANN, 1945; "Napier Nomad," 1954). Also under NACA Reports: *12th, 1926* (PATON and KEMPER).

Aircraft Power Before 1900

VILLENEUVE, A. HUREAU. Rapport sur l'Exposition Aéronautique de 1868. *L'Aéronautique*, vol. 1, no. 7 (July 1868), pp. 51–53; no. 8 (August 1868), pp. 67–75; no. 9 (September 1868), pp. 83–88; no. 10 (October 1868), pp. 99–105; no. 11 (November 1868) pp. 115–120; no. 12 (December 1868), pp. 131–135; vol. 2, no. 1 (January 1869), pp. 3–6; no. 2 (February 1869), pp. 19–22; no. 3 (March 1869), pp. 35–39; no. 4 (April 1869), pp. 51–55; no. 6 (June 1869), pp. 83–88; no. 8 (August 1869). pp. 115–118. Covers the aero exposition at London, 1868.

PÉNAUD, ALPHONSE. Aéroplane automoteur. *L'Aéronaute*, vol. 5, no. 1 (January 1872), pp. 2–9. Use of india rubber for model propulsion.

HAENLIEN, PAUL. Ueber den Treibapparat bei Luftschiffen. *Zeitschrift fur Luftfahrt*, vol. 1, no. 8, 1882, pp. 240–244. Author made world's first flight with an internal combustion engine (dirigible balloon).

TISSANDIER, GASTON. Propulseur dynamo-electrique pour aérostat elongé. *L'Aéronautique*, vol. 16, no. 5 (May 1883), pp. 83–88. Electric motor with bichromate of potassium battery. Used in flight of dirigible airship.

GOUPIL, ALEXANDRE L. *La Locomotion aérienne*. Charleville, France: Impr. de A. Pouillard, 1884. 112 pp., illus., incl. foldout diagrs.

DEGRAFFIGNY, HENRI. Les moteurs légers; applicable à la navigation aérienne. *L'Aérophile*, vol. 2, no. 6–7 (June–July 1894), pp. 128–134. Contemporary steam, gas, electric, and compressed-air engines.

Engines 1900–1913

Airship after buyer; inventors of North Carolina box kite machine want government to purchase it. *The New York Times* (Saturday, December 26, 1903), p. 1, col. 7. Brief notice of Wright Brothers' 1903 flights. A 4-inch item, at the top of the page, which refers to the great day at Kitty Hawk. (Reproduced here, fig. 10.)

The failure of Langley's Aerodrome. *Scientific American*, vol. 89, no. 16 (October 17, 1903), p. 272, illus.

By motor through the air. *The Automobile* (London, November 28, 1903), vol. 1, pp. 80–84.

HARRIMAN, J. EINERY, JR. Mechanical flight. *Journal of the Association of Engineering Societies*, vol. 33, no. 2 (August 1904), pp. 43–53, illus.

Santos-DuMont, Alberto. The future of the airship. *Outlook*, vol 77, no. 1 (May 7, 1904), pp. 52–53. In this item he remarks, "Abandon the balloon and build a flying machine, never!" Later, he did!

Eight-cylinder "Antionette" motor for aeroplane. *Engineering*, vol. 82 (November 30, 1906), p. 703, illus., drg.

Light-weight gasoline motors for aeronautical work. *Scientific American Supplement*, Vol. 62, no. 1612 (November 24, 1906), pp. 25–33, illus. Levavasseur's Antionette V, liquid-cooled engine.

Samuel Pierpont Langley. *Scientific American*, vol. 94, no. 10 (March 10, 1906), pp. 207, 211. Obituary.

The White Flyer—the motor driven aeroplane of the brothers Wright. *Automotor Journal*, vol. 11, no. 1 (January 1906), pp. 17–20, illus. An early account based on visits to Dayton by representatives of *L'Auto* of France. Discusses the question of secrecy by the Wrights. No mention of wing warping.

The Wright aeroplane and its performances. *Scientific American*, vol. 94, no. 14 (April 7, 1906), p. 291, illus.

Gasoline motors for aeronautical work. *Scientific American Supplement*, vol. 65, no. 1672 (January 11, 1908), pp. 28–30. Illus., drg. Survey of French engines: Dufaux, Farcot, R.E.P., Renault, Dutheil & Chalmers, and others.

Howland, Harold J. The sons of Daedalus. *Outlook*, vol. 90, no. 3 (September 26, 1908), pp. 153–169. Illus. Summary of air navigation to date. Mentions Wright Brothers' first flight and first flight of Wilbur at Le Mans, August 11, 1908.

Types of recent foreign flying machines. *Scientific American Supplement*, vol. 65, no. 1680 (March 14, 1908), pp. 172–174, illus.

Wright, Orville and Wilbur. The Wright brothers' aëroplane. *Century*, vol. 76, no. 5 (September 1908), pp. 641–650, illus. First public account by the Wright brothers; illustrated with photos of gliding and power flights.

The Aero Exhibition. *Engineering*, vol. 87 (March 26, 1909), pp. 413–415, 418, drgs. Olympia aero show of 1909.

Dantin, C. Moteurs thermiques: Les Moteurs à explosion légers pour dirigibles et aéroplanes. *Génie Civil*, vol. 55, no. 1408 (June 5, 1909), pp. 111–114; no. 1409 (June 12, 1909), pp. 125–129; and no. 1410 (June 19, 1909), pp. 150–156, illus., diagrs., finely done drawings, and footnote references in the text.

Fournier, L. Le Moteur d'aviation Clement-Bayard. *Cosmos* (Paris), vol. 58, no. 1259 (March 13, 1909), pp. 284–287. Illus. Describes the Clement-Bayard engine.

Nesfield, Albert C. The design of engines for aeroplanes. *Aeronautics*, vol. 2, no. 3 (March 1909), pp. 22–23; no. 4 (April 1909), pp. 38–40; no. 5 (May 1909), pp. 49–50; no. 6 (June 1909), pp. 60–61. Illus., drgs.

The Paris Aviation Exhibition. *Engineering* (October 1, 1909), vol. 88, pp. 452, 456–458, illus., tab. data.

Rumpler, E. Motoren für Luftfahrzeuge. *Vereines Deutsche Zeitschrift des Ingenieure*, vol. 53, no. 12 (March 20, 1909), pp. 441–448; no. 13 (March 27, 1909), pp. 487–492; no. 14 (April 3, 1909), pp. 532–538; and no. 15 (April 10, 1909), pp. 578–584. Illus; many excellent drgs.

VORREITER, A. VON. Neue Flugmotore. *Zeitschrift fur Flugtechnik und Motorluftschriffarlet*, Heft 3 und 4, 1910, pp. 41–44. Panhard, Wunderlich, Esnault Pelterie, Clement-Bayard, Miese, Bertin engines.

Alexandre Anzani. *L'Aérophile*, vol. 19, no. 1 (January 1, 1911), p. 5. Anzani fan, radial, air-cooled engine.

Le Moteur Renault. *L'Aérophile*, vol. 19, no. 6 (March 15, 1911), pp. 128–129, illus., drgs.

Le Nouveau Moteur R.E.P. *L'Aérophile*, vol. 19, No. 8 (April 15, 1911), pp. 177–179, illus.

Louis Seguin. *L'Aérophile*, vol. 20, no. 4 (February 15, 1912), p. 73. Relates to Gnome rotary, air-cooled engine of which Seguin was the designer.

Les Moteurs à l'Exposition. *L'Aérophile*, vol. 20, no. 22 (November 1, 1912), pp. 512–517, illus., drgs. Paris air show, 1912.

See also under History and Technology ("Ellehammer," 1966; McSURELY, 1953; MEYER, 1961; "On a Great Pioneer," 1922; VEAL, 1939).

Engines 1914-1919

MACCOULL, NEIL. Aeroplane engines. *Aerial Age Weekly*, vol. 1, no. 14 (June 21, 1915) pp. 322–323; no. 15 (June 28, 1915), pp. 346–347; no. 16 (July 5, 1915), pp. 372–373; no. 17 (July 12, 1915), pp. 406–407; no. 18 (July 19, 1915), pp. 426–427; no. 19 (July 26, 1915), pp. 450–451; no. 20 (August 2, 1915), p. 475; and no. 21 (August 9, 1915), pp. 498–499. Illus., drgs., tab. data.

———. Sturtevant motors. *Aerial Age Weekly*, vol. 1, no. 2 (March 29, 1915), pp. 33–34; and no. 7 (May 3, 1915), pp. 154–155. Illus., drgs., graph data.

———. American aeronautical engines; an important parallel between the development of the engines of the automobile and the airplane. *Aerial Age Weekly*, vol. 1, no. 1 (March 22, 1915), p. 7. Tab. data on 12 engines.

GRIFFITH, LEIGH M. Some notes on high-pressure aviation engines. *SAE Transactions*, vol. 12, pt. 1, 1917, 180–193. Includes discussion by Manly, Vincent, Maxim, Stout, and others.

LESCARBOURA, AUSTIN C. Bringing the Gnome engine to America; how this most intricate of aviation engines is being successfully manufactured in our country. *Scientific American*, vol. 16, no. 14 (April 7, 1917), pp. 374–375, illus., diagr.

PAGÉ, VICTOR W. Development of aviation engines. *Scientific American*, vol. 117, no. 14 (October 6, 1917), pp. 247, 258–259, illus., tab. data.

———. *Aviation engines*. 589 pp. illus. New York: Norman W. Henley Publishing Co., 1917. A good description of aircraft engine practice up to 1917. Details of some important early engines.

SHERBONDY, E. H. Aviation engine development. *SAE Transactions*, vol. 12, pt. 2, 1917, pp. 274–302, illus., drgs., tab. and graph data.

CHASE, HERBERT. Modern aeronautic engines. *SAE Transactions*, vol. 13, pt. 2, 1918, pp. 241–266, illus. A survey, heavily illustrated.

———. Aeronautic engines. *SAE Journal*, vol. 3, no. 2 (August 1918), pp. 147–152; and no. 3 (September 1918), pp. 205–208. Lavishly illustrated.

Durand, William F. Outstanding aeronautic problems. *SAE Journal*, vol. 3, no. 3 (September 1918), pp. 213–219; no. 4 (October 1918), pp. 280–284. Excellent general discussion.

Evolution of the aircraft engine. *Scientific American*, vol. 119, no. 14 (October 5, 1918), p. 270, tab. data.

How the Hispano-Suiza engine came to the forefront of aviation. *Scientific American*, vol. 118, no. 1 (January 6, 1918), pp. 7, 20.

Kettering, Charles F. The future of the airplane business. *SAE Transactions*, 1918, pt. 2, pp. 363–379. Interesting predictions by an eminent engineer of that time.

Lay, Donald McLeod. The Hispano-Suiza aircraft engine. *SAE Transactions*, vol. 13, pt. 2, 1918, 475–491. Illus. Also *SAE Journal*, vol. 3, no. 6 (December 1918), pp. 367–372.

The Liberty motor; Its checkered career and details of its construction. *Scientific American*, vol. 119, no. 23 (December 7, 1918), pp. 455, 466, illus., drg.

The true story of the Liberty motor. *Scientific American*, vol. 118, no. 22 (June 1, 1918), pp. 500, 515.

Upton, G. B. Airplane performance determined by engine performance. *SAE Journal*, vol. 3, no. 4 (October 1918), pp. 275–279.

Colvin, Fred H. How Ford built Liberty motors. *American Machinist*, vol. 51, no. 23 (December 18, 1919), pp. 1037–1041, illus.

Douglas, Donald W. The airplane as a commercial possibility. *SAE Transactions*, vol. 14, pt. 2, 1919, pp. 444–462. Strong emphasis on need for engine development.

A German view of the Liberty engine. *The Aeroplane*, vol. 17, no. 14 (October 1, 1919), Aeronautical Engineering Supplement, p. 1266.

The 200 h.p. Mercedes engine. *SAE Journal*, vol. 5, no. 2 (August 1919), p. 191.

The 450 h.p. Napier "Lion" engine. *SAE Journal*, vol. 5, no. 6 (December 1919), pp. 430–432. Includes 2 fine cross-sectional drawings.

Sayers, W. H. Aerial propulsion. *The Aeroplane*, vol. 17, August 13, 1919, pp. 593–594, and August 27, 1919, pp. 809–810.

Smith, John W. Fixed radial cylinder engines. *SAE Transactions*, vol. 14, pt. 1, 1919, pp. 294–303. The Smith 10-cyl 400-hp, radial, air-cooled engine.

Vincent, J. G. The Liberty aircraft engine. *SAE Transactions*, vol. 14, pt. 1 (1919), pp. 385–432, illus., drgs. in text and large fold-out drg., tab. and graph data.

Wardrop, G. Douglas. The Liberty engine. *The Aeroplane*, vol. 16, January 29, 1919, pp. 480–482, 499–500; February 5, 1919, pp. 582, 599; and February 12, 1919, pp. 676–678, 680, 697. Illus.

See also under History and Technology (Angle, 1921; Dickey, 1968). Under *Engines 1920–1924* (Heller, 1920). *Engines 1930–1934* ("The Hispano-Suiza Aero Engines," 1934). Also under NACA Reports: *8th, 1923* (Sparrow).

Engines 1920-1924

Abell, C. F. Airship machinery, past experience and future requirements. *Journal of the Royal Aeronautical Society*, vol. 24 no. 113 (May 1920), pp. 250–268.

Bauman, A. Progress made in the construction of giant airplanes in Germany during the war. *NACA Technical Note*, no. 29, 1920, 11 pp., tab. data.

LOENING, GROVER C. Engine shape as affecting airplane operation. *SAE Transactions*, vol. 15, pt. 1, 1920, pp. 577–590, illus., drgs., tab. and graph data.

NOACK, W. G. Tests of the Daimler D–IVa engine at a high altitude test bench. *NACA Technical Note*, no. 15, 1920, 20 pp., extensive graph and tab. data.

SCHWAGER, OTTO. Development of German aircraft engines. *Aviation*, vol. 9, October 1, 1920, pp. 161–164, and October 15, 1920, pp. 186–189.

——. Recent efforts and experiments in the construction of aviation engines. *NACA Technical Note*, no. 12, 1920, 18 pp., graph and tab. data.

CHORLTON, ALAN E. L. Aero engines. *Journal of the Royal Society of Arts* [London], vol. 69, no. 3589 (September 2, 1921), pp. 689–705; no. 3590 (September 9, 1921), pp. 707–724; and no. 3591 (September 16, 1921), pp. 725–740. Well illus., by many fine drawings.

Development of an American pursuit engine. *Aviation*, vol. 11, no. 26 (December 26, 1921), pp. 735–738. The Hispano-Suiza as developed under license in the U.S.A.

HELLER, A. The 300 h.p. Benz aircraft engine. Transl. from *Zeitschrift des Vereines Deutsche Ingenieure* (1920). *NACA Technical Note*, no. 34, 1921, 17 pp. Includes cross-sectional and several detail drgs.

SPARROW, S. W. High thermal efficiency in airplane service. *NACA Technical Note*, no. 39, 1921, 7 pp., drgs.

Tests of the 450 h.p. Bristol Jupiter engine. *Aviation*, vol. 11, no. 24 (December 12, 1921), pp. 685–686, graph and tab. data.

WARE, MARSDEN. Effect of the reversal of air flow upon the discharge coefficient of Durley orifices. *NACA Technical Note*, no. 40, 1921, 14 pp., diagrs., graph data.

HERON, S. D. Air cooled cylinder design. *SAE Transactions*, vol. 17, pt. 1, 1922, pp. 347–430, illus., drgs., graph and tab. data. Contains history and detail design.

Navy changes in Liberty motor responsible for improvement in Navy plane operations. *Aerial Age*, vol. 15, no. 18 (September 1922), pp. 455, 478.

TAYLOR, C. FAYETTE. Recent aircraft engine developments. *SAE Transactions*, vol. 17, Pt. 1, 1922, pp. 872–881, illus.

CHRISTIANSEN, O. C. Test of Armstrong Siddeley "Jaguar" 14-cylinder radial aviation engine rated at 320 h.p. at 1500 r.p.m. U.S. Army Air Service (Engineering Division, McCook Field), *Report*, no. 2218, July 16, 1923. 53 pp., illus., diagrs., graph data.

HERON, SAMUEL D. Exhaust valves and guides for aircraft engines. U.S. Army Air Service (Engineering Division, McCook Field), *Report*, no. 2328, September 4, 1923. 28 pp., Illus., diagrs., graph data. Record of early development work on internal cooling through the use of "salts," sodium and potassium nitrate mixture.

LEIGHTON, BRUCE G., LT., USN. Recent developments in aircraft and engines in the Navy. *SAE Transactions*, vol. 18, Pt. 1, 1923, pp. 862–887, illus., drgs., graph data.

MOFFET, WILLIAM A., RADM., USN. The aeronautical engine: Some differences between the airship and airplane power plant. *U.S. Air Services*, vol. 8, no. 3 (March 1923), pp. 13–15.

ANGLE, GLENN D. Progress Toward 1000 hp. aircraft engines. *Aviation* (February 25, 1924), vol. 16, pp. 198–200, illus. Author was in charge of engine design, U.S. Army Air Service.

MEAD, GEORGE J. Airplane Engine Designing for Reliability. *SAE Transactions*, vol. 19, Pt. 1, 1924, pp. 695-717, illus., drgs., diagrs., graph data.

See also under History and Technology (HOURWICH and FOSTER, 1925; LAWRANCE, 1922; Vincent, 1922).

Engines 1925-1929

BOEDECKER, K. J. The economy of air cooling. *Aviation*, vol. 18, no. 18 (May 4, 1925), pp. 492-493. Mostly about the Wright J series.

McCORD, CHARLES G., LT., USN. Aeronautical Engine Laboratory, Naval Aircraft Factory, Philadelphia. *Journal of the American Society of Naval Engineers* (May 1925), vol. 37, pp. 275-305.

The makers of Napier engines. *Aviation*, vol. 19, no. 17 (October 26, 1925), pp. 586-588 illus. Napier Lion and the Schneider Cup.

The new Packard aircraft engines; detailed description of the latest aircraft engines produced by the Packard Motor Car Co. *Aviation*, vol. 18, no. 19 (May 11, 1925), pp. 517-520, illus.

Pratt and Whitney Aircraft Co. formed to manufacture aircraft engines. *Aviation*, vol. 19, no. 5 (August 3, 1925), p. 121.

TAYLOR, C. FAYETTE. The design of air-cooled cylinders. *Aviation*, vol. 18, no. 23 (June 8, 1925), pp. 634-636; no. 24 (June 15, 1925), pp. 664-667. Drgs., illus., tab. data.

WILSON, EUGENE E., CDR., USN. Aircraft engine design. *NACA Technical Note*, no. 211, 1925. 30 pp., illus., diagrs., graph data. A good survey, as of 1924.

Armstrong-Siddeley in field with light air-cooled aircraft engine. *Automotive Industries*, vol. 55, no. 18 (October 28, 1926), p. 746. Graph data on Armstrong-Siddeley 65-hp Genet.

DENHAM, ATHEL F. Cam is used instead of crank train in radial airplane engine. *Automotive Industries*, vol. 54, no. 21 (May 27, 1926), pp. 891-893, illus., drgs. The Fairchild Caminez engine.

DINGER, H. C., CAPT., USN. The development of the Wright air-cooled aviation engine. *Journal of the American Society of Naval Engineers*, vol. 38, no. 4 (November 1926), pp. 856-878, illus.

The Fairchild-Caminez engine; an airplane engine designed along new lines and embodying entirely new principles successfully tested in flight. *Aviation*, vol. 20, no. 21 (May 24, 1926), pp. 788-791, illus., drgs.

JONES, E. T. The development of the Wright Whirlwind, type J-5, aircraft engine. *SAE Transactions*, vol. 21, pt. 2, 1926, pp. 847-866, illus., drgs., graph data.

MEAD, GEORGE J. Wasp and Hornet radial air-cooled aeronautic engines. *SAE Transactions*, vol. 21, pt. 2 (1926), pp. 867-886, illus.

NUTT, ARTHUR. Progress in aircraft engine design. *SAE Transactions*, vol. 21, pt. 2 (1926), pp. 887-910, illus., graph data.

Pratt & Whitney anniversary; two high powered radial engines successfully produced within the year. *Aviation*, vol. 21, no. 6 (August 9, 1926), pp. 246-249.

WILSON, EUGENE E., CDR., USN. Air-cooled engines in naval aircraft. *SAE Transactions*, vol. 21, pt. 2 (1926), pp. 812-846.

The trend of aircraft engine development. *Journal of the American Society of Naval Engineers* (February 1926), vol. 38, pp. 130-143, illus.

Cam engine passes fifty hour test; Fairchild-Caminez Engine Corp. Development announced as an approved type. *Aviation*, vol. 23, no. 1 (July 4, 1927), pp. 20-21, illus.

CARTER, B. C. Dynamic forces in aircraft engines. *Journal of the Royal Aeronautical Society* (April 1927), vol. 31, pp. 277-328, illus., drgs., graph data.

The Continental single sleeve valve engine. *Aviation*, vol. 22, no. 17 (April 25, 1927), p. 826.

Engines at the Paris aero show. *Aviation*, vol. 22, no. 3 (January 17, 1927), pp. 122-129, illus., tab. data.

Performance of Fairchild airplane engine improved. *Automotive Industries*, vol. 57, no. 5 (July 30, 1927), p. 160. Fairchild Caminez engine.

WILSON, EUGENE E., CDR., USN. American air-cooled aircraft engines. *Journal of the American Society of Naval Engineers* (August 1927), vol. 39, pp. 533-543, illus.

BOURDON, M. W. Huge air-cooled airplane engine develops nearly 800 B.H.P. *Automotive Industries*, vol. 58, no. 24 (June 16, 1928), pp. 920-921, illus., graph data. Armstrong-Siddeley radial, air-cooled engine.

CLEMENTS, BISHOP. The metallurgy of aircraft engines. ASME, *Transactions*, vol. 50, 1928, pp. 1-2.

FOKKER, A. H. G. Single-engine versus multi-engine airplanes. *SAE Transactions*, vol. 23, 1928, pp. 223-227.

MEAD, GEORGE J. The "Wasp" series B engine. *Aviation* (June 11, 1928), vol. 24, pp. 1678-1679, 1703-1704, illus.

WOOLSON, L. M. The Packard X, 24-cylinder 1500 h.p. water-cooled aircraft engine. *SAE Transactions*, vol. 23, 1928, pp. 493-504, illus., drgs., diagrs.

Wright "Whirlwind" Engine. *Journal of the Franklin Institute*, vol. 206, no. 5 (November 1928), report 2890, pp. 681-687, illus.

BROOKS, DONALD B. Horsepower correction for atmospheric humidity. *SAE Transactions*, vol. 24, 1929, pp. 273-279, graph data.

Continental 7-cylinder aircraft engine develops 150 H.P. *Automotive Industries*, vol. 60, no. 10 (March 9, 1929), pp. 404-406, illus., sectional drg.

HERON, S. D. The in-line air-cooled engine. *SAE Transactions*, vol. 24, 1929, pp. 423-434, illus., drgs., diagrs. Especially the air-cooled Liberty variant, the Wright V-1460, among others.

LEIGHTON, BRUCE G. Races—the test-block for aviation. *Aviation*, vol. 27, no. 8 (August 24, 1929), pp. 393-394.

Lycoming develops aero engine of radial type in two models. *Automotive Industries*, vol. 61, no. 9 (August 31, 1929), pp. 295-297, illus., tab. data. The 9-cylinder R-645 and 7-cylinder R-500.

STOUT, R. CHEYNE. The development of the Cirrus engine. *U.S. Air Services*, vol. 14, no. 4 (April 1929), pp. 53-54.

TAYLOR, C. FAYETTE. A study of the engines exhibited at the Olympia aero show. *Aviation* (August 31, 1929), vol. 27, pp. 456-463, illus., tab. data.

PAGÉ, VICTOR W. *Modern Aviation Engines*, 1908 pp., 2 vol., illus. New York: Norman W. Henley Publishing Co., 1929.

See also under History and Technology (GEISSE, 1928; "Lindbergh's Wright Whirlwind . . . ," 1927; MEAD, 1925 and 1929; RICARDO, 1930; TAYLOR, 1926).

Engines 1930-1934

HALL, E. S. Engines having the cylinders parallel to the shaft. *SAE Journal*, vol. 46, no. 4 (October 1930), pp. 408–412, 476. Traces historical development, including drgs. from several patents.

LOTT, E. P., and SMITH, W. L. The operator's airplane and engine requirements. *SAE Journal*, vol. 46, no. 4 (October 1930), pp. 393–402, 407.

LYON, A. J. Aluminum alloys of aircraft engine piston and cylinder heads. ASME, *Transactions*, vol. 52, 1930, pp. 257–269, illus., diagrs.

SETTLE, T. G. W., Lt., USN. Airship engines. U.S. Naval Institute, *Proceedings*, vol. 56, no. 8 (August 1930), pp. 745–747.

BANKS, F. RODWELL. The evolution of a Schneider engine. *The Aeroplane* (October 7, 1931), vol. 41, pp. 864, 866, 868, 870, 782, illus. Rolls-Royce model R.

CHILTON, ROLAND. Air-cooled cylinder-head design. *SAE Transactions*, vol. 26, 1931, pp. 542–545.

New crankcase reduces weight of Continental aircraft engine. *Automotive Industries*, vol. 64, no. 12 (March 21, 1931), p. 483. Model A–70 radial.

Rolls-Royce, Ltd.; D. Napier & Son, Ltd. *The Aeroplane* (September 9, 1931), vol. 41, pp. 632, 634, 636. British Schneider racers' power plants.

TAYLOR, PHILIP B. Increasing the thrust horsepower from radial air-cooled engines. *SAE Transactions*, vol. 26, 1931, pp. 531–541, illus., diagrs. At this time Taylor was chief engineer at Wright Aero.

DIETRICH, OTTO, and LEHR, ERNST. Das Dehnungslinienverfahren ein Mittel zur Bestimmung der für die Bruchsicherheit bei Wechselbeanspruchung massgebenden Spannungsverteilung. *Zeitschrift des Vereines Deutscher Ingenieure*, vol. 76, no. 41 (October 8, 1932), pp. 973–982, illus. This article introduced the very important method of exploring stresses in engine parts by the brittle-lacquer technique. It has had a profoundly beneficial effect on engine development since that time.

LOWES, JOSEPH E. The Pratt & Whitney twin Wasp Jr. engine. *Journal of the American Society of Naval Engineers*, vol. 44, no. 3 (August 1932), pp. 371–373.

ANGLE, GLENN D. Developments in high-powered aircraft engines. *Aero Digest*, vol. 23, no. 4 (October 1933), pp. 41–44, and no. 5 (November 1933), pp. 46–47, illus. Emphasis is upon liquid-cooled engines.

Comparison of recent European and American military aircraft engines. *Interavia*, no. 41 (August 24, 1933), pp. 1–2, and no. 42 (August 28, 1933), pp. 1–2.

FEDDEN, A. H. R. Next decade's aero engines will be advanced but not radical. *SAE Transactions*, vol. 28, 1933, pp. 377–401, illus., drgs., diagrs. Draws heavily upon Bristol's experience. Fedden was chief engineer for the engines of the Bristol Aeroplane Company.

High-output engines: A British point of view and an American one. *Aviation*, vol. 32, no. 10 (October 1933), pp. 321–323.

HILL, HENRY C. 400-hour endurance test of the Wright Whirlwind R–760E–1. *Aero Digest*, vol. 23, no. 3 (September 1933), pp. 50–51.

Pratt & Whitney two-row engine development. *Aviation Engineering*, vol. 8, no. 4 (April 1933), pp. 17–18, 27, illus.

TAYLOR, E. S. Radial engines: Their power and frontal area. *Aviation*, vol. 32, no. 7 (July 1933), pp. 201–202.

The Hispano-Suiza aero engines. *Interavia*, no. 166 (November 8, 1934), pp. 1–6.

TAYLOR, C. FAYETTE. Power plants in 1933. *Aviation*, vol. 34, no. 1 (January 1934), pp. 19–20.

See also under History and Technology (DAVY and RICHARDS, 1930).

Engines 1935-1939

Pratt & Whitney E Hornet, 750 h.p. engine. *Aero Digest*, vol. 26, no. 1 (January 1935), pp. 42–43.

CHATFIELD, CHARLES H. Pratt & Whitney's development of the two-row radial aircraft engine. *Aero Digest*, vol. 26, no. 4 (April 1935), pp. 32–34, illus.

Wright series F–50 Cyclone engines. *Aero Digest*, vol. 26, no. 6 (June 1935), pp. 30, 32, 36, illus.

Bristol Pegasus Engine. *Automobile Engineer*, vol. 26, no. 346 (June 1936), pp. 221–224. Bristol poppet-valve engine with aluminum heads. Successor to the "Jupiter."

LÜRENBAUM, KARL. Vibration of crankshaft-propeller Systems. *SAE Transactions*, vol. 31, 1936, pp. 469–472.

TAYLOR, E. S. Eliminating crankshaft torsional vibration in radial aircraft engines. *SAE Transactions*, vol. 31, 1936, pp. 81–89. Theory and practice of tuned absorbers.

WOOD, H. Liquid-cooled aero engines. *SAE Transactions*, vol. 31, 1936, pp. 267–287, 400, 424, illus., tab. and graph data. Relates chiefly to the Rolls-Royce Kestral engine.

1,000 h.p. Wright Cyclone. *Aero Digest*, vol. 29, no. 3 (September 1936), pp. 32, 35, illus.

YOUNG, RAYMOND W. Air-cooled radial aircraft engine performance possibilities. *SAE Transactions*, vol. 31, 1936, pp. 234–256, illus., drgs., diagrs., graph data. Relates chiefly to Wright Aero's models.

Accent on the aspirate; some glimpses of Napier 'H'-shaped engines in production. *Flight*, vol. 31, no. 1485 (June 10, 1937), Engineering Supplement, pp. a, b, c.

Allison 1,000 h.p. chemically-cooled model 1710 engine. *Aero Digest*, vol. 30, no. 6 (June 1937), pp. 50, 88–89. This engine was a close copy of the Rolls-Royce Merlin.

FEDDEN, A. H. R. Trend of air-cooled aero engines—the next five years. *SAE Transactions*, vol. 32, 1937, pp. 437–454, 467, illus., drgs., graph and tab. data. References are mostly to British and Bristol developments.

GREGORY, A. T. Features of the in-line air-cooled aircraft engine. *SAE Transactions*, vol. 32, 1937, pp. 473–482, illus., drgs., tab. and graph data. Fairchild SGV–770 Ranger engine. Gregory was chief engineer of Ranger.

LOMBARD, A. E., Jr. How many engines? The question of power plant sub-division can't be solved by the old eenie, meenie, meinie moe formula. *Aviation*, vol. 36, no. 7 (July 1937), pp. 30–31, 63–64, 67–68. Includes footnote references.

MEAD, GEORGE J. Aircraft power plant trends. *SAE Transactions*, vol. 32, 1937, pp. 455–467, illus., drgs., graph data. More on Pratt and Whitney engines.

The coming of the sleeve valve. *Aircraft Engineering*, vol. 9, no. 102 (August 1937), pp. 203–204. Bristol sleeve-valve engine.

How the sleeve valve works. *The Aeroplane*, vol. 52, no. 1362 (June 30, 1937), p. 816, illus. Bristol sleeve-valve engine.

CARRY, WILLIAM J. Latest twelve cylinder Ranger engines. *Aero Digest*, vol. 32, no. 4 (April 1938), pp. 46, 48, 90–91, illus., graph data. Ranger vertical and V, air-cooled engine.

A new air-cooled motor. *The Aeroplane*, vol. 54, no. 1413 (June 22, 1938), pp. 776–778, illus., drgs., phantom view. DeHavilland 525-hp Gypsy 4-cylinder vertical for light planes.

DRAPER, C. S. Gas pressure torque in radial engines. *Journal of the Aeonautical Sciences*, vol. 6, no. 1 (November 1938), pp. 1–6, graph data, footnote refs.

FEDDEN, A. H. R. The single sleeve as a valve mechanism for the aircraft engine. *SAE Transactions*, vol. 33, 1938, pp. 349–365, illus., drgs., diagrs., graph data.

HAZEN, R. M., and MONTEITH, O. V. Torsional vibration of in-line aircraft engines. *SAE Transactions*, vol. 33, 1938, pp. 335–341, graph data. The Allison V–1710 engine.

Seven cylinder Lycoming; new R–530–D series supplements established line of nine cylinder engines. *Aviation*, vol. 37, no. 1 (January 1938), P. 38, illus., specs.

Perseus production. *The Aeroplane*, vol. 44, no. 1412 (June 15, 1938), pp. 751–752, illus., drgs.

The first sleeve valve engine in production. *The Aeroplane*, vol. 44, no. 1403 (April 13, 1938), p. 453, illus. Bristol Perseus XII.

TAYLOR, E. S., and BROWNE, K. A. Vibration isolation of aircraft power plants. *Journal of the Aeronautical Sciences*, vol. 6, no. 2 (December 1938), pp. 43–49, diagrs., drgs., graph data, footnote refs.

BENTLEY, G. P. Vibration of radial aircraft engines. *Journal of the Aeronautical Sciences*, vol. 6, no. 7 (May 1939), pp. 278–283, and no. 8 (June 1939), pp. 333–341, diagrs., tab., and graph data, footnote refs.

BROWNE, K. A. Dynamic suspension—a method of aircraft-engine mounting. *SAE Transactions*, vol. 34, 1939, pp. 185–192. Describes 6-degree rubber mounting for radial engines.

KAMPER, CARLTON. Aircraft engine research of the National Adivsory Committee for Aeronautics. *Journal of the Aeronautical Sciences*, vol. 6, no. 12 (October 1939), pp. 479–484, illus., diagrs., graph data, footnote refs.

See also under History and Technology ("Search of Archives Reveals Interesting Engine Histories," 1938).

Piston Engines 1940 and After

COLWELL, A. T. Modern aircraft valves. *SAE Transactions*, vol. 35, 1940, pp. 147–152. Comprehensive description of current practice.

DEFOREST, A. V., and ELLIS, GREER. Brittle lacquers as an aid to stress analysis. *Journal of the Aeronautical Sciences*, vol. 7, no. 5 (March 1940), pp. 205–208, illus., footnote refs. Adaptation of Diedrick and Lehr work in the United States.

The development of sodium cooling of exhaust valves. *Automotive Industries*, vol. 82, no. 9 (May 1, 1940), pp. 417–418, diagrs. R.A.E. trials of water and mercury in 1913. Midgeley and Kettering patent on causing wetting of steel surface by mercury, 1917. Salt cooling by Heron, 1923, first used in Wright J–5 engine, 1926. Metallic sodium followed.

Lycoming geared 75 h.p. engine. *Aviation*, vol. 39, no. 1 (January 1940), p. 50, illus., specs. Four-cylinder-opposed geared engine for light airplanes.

Lycoming 12-cylinder horizontally opposed engine. *Aviation*, vol. 30, no. 6 (June 1940), p. 114. A very brief item.

MOREHOUSE, HAROLD E. Light aircraft engine developments. *Journal of the Aeronautical Sciences*, vol. 8, no. 10 (August 1941), pp. 393–400, illus., diagrs., exploded views, graph data. Includes some very small engines, never widely used.

BROWNBACK, HENRY L. Development of the radial engine for military uses. *Automotive Industries*, vol. 84, no. 4 (February 15, 1941), 156–160, illus., degs. Historical account of Anzani fan and radial air-cooled engines. Brownback built small engines in the United States, based on Anzani practices.

HAZEN, R. M. The Allison aircraft engine development. *SAE Transactions*, vol. 36, 1941, pp. 488–500, illus., drgs., diagrs., graph and tab. data.

YOUNG, RAYMOND W. Mercedes-Benz DB–601A aircraft engine: Design features and performance characteristics. *SAE Transactions*, vol. 36, 1941, pp. 409–431, illus., drgs., graph data. Three excellent British phantom view drgs. from *The Aeroplane*.

The B.M.W. 801 aero-engine. *Aircraft Engineering*, vol. 14, no. 162 (August 1942), pp. 223–227, illus., schematic drgs.

German BMW 801 Engine. *Automotive Industries*, vol. 89, no. 3 (August 1, 1943), p. 44. Phantom view drawing from *The Aeroplane*.

CAVÉ, MYLES V. Design details of the BMW–801A engine. *Aviation*, vol. 42, no. 11 (November 1942), pp. 228–229, 291–294, 296, and no. 12 (December 1942), pp. 256–257, 259, illus. Accompanied by excellent British drawings from *Flight* magazine.

OLDBERG, SIDNEY, and BALL, THOMAS M. Design features of the Junkers 211B aircraft engine. *SAE Transactions*, vol. 50, 1942, pp. 465–483, illus., diagrs., graph and extensive tab. data.

OVEYS, W. G. Some notes on design features of the Mitsubishi Kinsei engine. *SAE Transactions*, vol. 50, 1942, pp. 253–266, illus.

SHEFFIELD, F. C. The B.M.W. 801A; details of Germany's latest twin-row radial power plant. *Flight*, vol. 42, no. 1755 (August 13, 1942), pp. 169–173, and no. 1756 (August 20, 1942), pp. 201–202, illus., drgs., phantom view, exploded views.

YOSHIKAWA, HARUO. Japan's Power Units. *Flight*, vol. 42, no. 1751 (July 16, 1942), pp. 70–72, illus. Author was Japanese naval attache, Berlin. His article is translated from *Luftwissen*.

CARTER, B. C., and FORSHAW, J. R. Torsiograph observations on a Merlin II engine, using a serrated condenser pick-up with five different pitch settings of the propeller blades. *Reports and Memoranda*, Aero Research Committee, no. 1983, July 1943.

Lycoming "packaged power" unit. *Automotive Industries*, vol. 89, no. 10 (November 15, 1943), p. 23, illus. A 775-lb, 162-hp, horizontally opposed model.

ELLOR, J. E. The development of the Merlin engine. *SAE Transactions*, vol. 52 (1944), pp. 385–392.

FEDDEN, A. H. R. Aircraft power plant—past and future. *Journal of the Royal Aeronautical Society* (October 1944), vol. 48, pp. 397–459, illus., drgs., diagrs., graph data. This was the 32nd Wilbur Wright memorial lecture. Also in *Flight*, vol. 45, no. 1849 (June 1, 1944), pp. 578–583, and no. 1850 (June 8, 1944), pp. 611–615, illus., drgs., phantom views, graph data.

GERDAN, DIMITRIUS. Late developments of the Allison aircraft engine. *SAE Transactions*, vol. 53, 1945, pp. 95–102, illus., drgs., graph data.

HERRMANN, KARL L. Cam engines for aircraft. *Aero Digest*, vol. 48, no. 1 (January 1945), pp. 100–101, illus.

New Continental aircraft engines. *Automotive Industries*, vol. 93, no. 12 (December 15, 1945), pp. 31, 92, 94, illus., tab. data. Models A–100, C–115, and C–125.

Ranger air-cooled, in-line engine. *Aero Digest*, vol. 49, no. 5 (June 1, 1915), pp. 72–76, 136, 138, illus., drgs., phantom view.

ANDERSON, R. G. Improving engine parts by direct measurement of strain. *SAE Transactions*, vol. 54, 1946, pp. 466–475. Extensive graph data.

LOVESAY, A. C. Development of the Rolls-Royce Merlin from 1939 to 1945. *Aircraft Engineering*, vol. 18, no. 209 (July 1946), pp. 218–226. Brilliantly illustrated with numerous cross-sections, schematics, and phantom view drawings.

BANKS, F. R. The art of the aviation engine. *Flight*, vol. 53, no. 2055 (May 13, 1948), pp. 530–531, 534, illus. Discussion of development time of various types of aircraft engines. Summary of the first Louis Bleriot lecture, given before the A.F.I.T.A. in Paris.

Napier Nomad: An engine of outstanding efficiency. *Flight*, vol. 65, no. 2362 (April 30, 1954), pp. 543–551, illus., drgs., fold-out phantom view, graph data.

See also under History and Technology (ANGLE, ed., *Aerosphere*, 1939–1943; "The Aviation Industry," 1952; BANKS, 1950; HERON, 1961; HOBBS, 1954; SCHLAIFER and HERON, 1950; "The Two R's . . . Rolls Royce Aero Engines," 1954; WILKINSON, 1944–).

Steam Engines

Flying machine work and the $\frac{1}{6}$ I.H.P. steam motor weighing 3¼ lbs. *Journal of the Royal Society of New South Wales*, 1892, p. 170.

WILSON, EUGENE E., CDR., USN. Steam power plants in aircraft. *NACA Technical Note*, no. 239, 1926, 32 pp., fold-out diagr., bibl. of 4 items. Discusses the general findings of the Navy's Bureau of Steam Engineering's Committee on Experimental Power, ca. 1922.

CADDELL, ALFRED M. Steam power for aircraft. *Aero News and Mechanics* (June–July 1930), pp. 26–27, 76, 79, 96, illus.

POLESINE, JOTTI DA BADIA. Il motore a vapore ed il suo impiego in aeronautica. *L'Aerotechnica*, vol. 11, no. 12 (December 1931), pp. 1555–1564. 19th-century experiments with steam engines for aircraft.

A steam driven airplane engine. *Scientific American*, vol. 149, no. 3 (September 1933), pp. 124–125, illus., diagr. Besler's steam engine in a Travelair airplane.

GRUBERG, V. L. Steam in the air; early attempts to use steam power in aircraft. *Flight*, vol. 42, no. 1753 (July 30, 1942), pp. 115–118, illus., drgs., diagrs.

MURPHY, FRANK L. Sir Hiram's steam-powered winged machines. *The Bee Hive*, vol. 33, no. 3 (summer 1958), pp. 7–11, illus.

Diesel Engines

WOOLSON, L. M. Diesel engines for aircraft. *SAE Transactions*, vol. 24, 1929, pp. 435–444. Packard diesel. First diesel to fly in heavier-than-air craft.

GASTERSTÄDT, J. Development of the Junkers diesel aircraft engine. A paper read before the Wissenschaftliche Gesellschaft fur Luftfahrt, trans. from *Automobiltechnische Zeitschrift* (January 10 and 20, 1930). *NACA Technical Memorandum*, no. 565, 1930, 25 pp., illus., drgs., diagrs. The most successful airplane diesel.

HEINZE, EDWIN P. A. Junkers develops diesel engine for aircraft use. *Automotive Industries*, vol. 62, no. 4 (January 25, 1930), pp. 121–122, illus.

WARNER, EDWARD P. The Packard aircraft diesel. *Aviation*, vol. 28, no. 14 (April 5, 1930), pp. 684–691, illus.

WOOLSON, L. M. The Packard diesel aircraft engine. *SAE Transactions*, vol. 25, 1930, pp. 236–248, illus. drgs.

Beardmore compression-ignition engines. *The Aeroplane* (April 29, 1931), vol. 40, p. 792.

Guiberson Diesel Engine. *Aviation*, vol. 31, no. 4 (April 1932), p. 195, drg.

MELCHIOR, FREDERICK. The Junkers "Jumo 4" heavy oil aircraft engine. *Journal of the American Society of Naval Engineers* (February 1932), vol. 44, pp. 104–109, illus.

WEBB, L. D., LCDR., USN. The diesels take the air. *U.S. Air Services*, vol. 17, no. 3 (March 1932), pp. 20–23.

The heavy oil aero engine in England. *Interavia*, no. 34 (July 31, 1933), pp. 1–3.

The progress of the heavy oil engine in France. *Interavia*, no. 18 (June 6, 1933), pp. 1–3, and no. 19 (June 8, 1933), pp. 1–2.

1200 h.p. diesel. *Aviation*, vol. 33, no. 8 (August 1934), pp. 271–272.

KENNEDY, JOHN B. A history of diesel engines. *Flying and Popular Aviation*, vol. 20, no. 3 (March 1937), pp. 36–38, 65.

Schwerölmotoren im Ozeanverkehr; Nordatlantikflüge der Deutschen Lufthansa. *Junkers-Nachrichten*, vol. 9, no. 11 (November 1938), pp. 281–285, illus. Use of the Junkers diesel engine in commercial airplanes.

VOGT, RICHARD. A family of motor mountings. *The Aeroplane*, vol. 44, no. 1414 (June 29, 1938), pp. 813–815, illus., drgs. Junkers Jumo diesel.

SAMMONS, HERBERT, and CHATTERTON, ERNEST. Napier Nomad aircraft diesel engine. *SAE Transactions*, vol. 63, 1955, pp. 107–131, illus., drgs., diagrs., graph data. Includes a phantom view of the engine. An experimental 24-cylinder 2-cycle turbo-compound diesel engine, the last try at this type.

MEYER, ROBERT B., Jr. The first airplane diesel engine: Packard model DR–980 of 1928. *Smithsonian Annals of Flight*, vol. 1, no. 2, 1964, 48 pp., illus., drgs., tab. data.

BLACKALL, T. E. Aircraft oil engines. *Air Pictorial*, vol. 28, no. 8 (August 1966), pp. 282–284, illus.

See also under History and Technology (WILKINSON, 1940). Under *Engines 1930–1934* (SETTLE, 1930). And under NACA Reports: *12th, 1926* (GARDINER); *14th, 1929* (JOACHIM and KEMPER); *17th, 1931* (ROTHROCK); *18th, 1932* (ROTHROCK); *20th, 1935* (SPANOGLE and WHITNEY); *22nd, 1936* (ROTHROCK and WALDRON, FOSTER); *23rd, 1937* (MOORE and COLLINS).

Jet, Rocket, and Turbine Engines

KOLEROFF, B. T. Possibility of reactive propulsion in air. *Aviation*, vol. 10, no. 21 (May 16, 1921), pp. 624–625.

Jet Propulsion in France. *The Aeroplane* (February 27, 1924), vol. 26, p. 176. The Melot engine.

Roy, Maurice. Propulsion by reaction. Transl. from *La Technique Aéronautique* (January 15, 1930). *NACA Technical Memorandum*, no. 571, 1930, 22 pp., drgs., graph data. Discusses solid and liquid-fueled rockets.

An internal combustion turbine. *The Aeroplane* (May 27, 1931), vol. 40, pp. 980, 982, 984, illus. The French Bertin engine.

Richardson, E. G. Jet propulsion for aircraft. *Journal of the Royal Aeronautical Society* (January 1931), vol. 35, pp. 29-36. Drgs. Emphasis is on rocket power.

Heizloftstrahltriebwerke. *Flugsport*, vol. 31, no. 1 (January 4, 1939), pp. 1-5; no. 2 (January 18, 1939), pp. 31-36; no. 3 (February 1, 1939), pp. 70-75; no. 4 (February 15, 1939), pp. 100-104. Illus., drgs. Jet propulsion, mostly historical.

Smith, G. Geoffrey. Possibilities of jet propulsion. *Flight*, vol. 40, September 11, 1941, pp. 155-158; September 25, 1941, pp. 190-192, 201; October 9, 1941, pp. 239-242. Illus. An excellent historical survey.

Thermal-air jet-propulsion. *Aircraft Engineering*, vol. 14, no. 156 (February 1942), pp. 32-39, illus., drgs. A translation of the *Flugsport* (1939) article.

Stemmer, J. The development of jet or rocket propulsion. *Journal of the Royal Aeronautical Society* (December 1943), vol. 47, pp. 500-518.

Whittle, Sir Frank. The early history of the Whittle jet-propulsion gas turbine. *The Aeroplane*, vol. 69, October 19, 1945, pp. 445-452; November 2, 1945, pp. 503-507; November 9, 1945, pp. 543-546. Illus. photos, diagrs., tab. data. Whittle developed and promoted the first successful jet engine with a centrifugal compressor. Concurrently, jets with axial compressors were developed in Germany.

Flagle, Charles D., and Godsey, Frank W., Jr. Gas turbine-propeller, jet drive and reciprocating engines. *Aero Digest*, vol. 50, no. 3 (August 1, 1945), pp. 60-63, 134, 137, graph data.

Zucrow, M. J. The rocket power plant. *SAE Transactions*, vol. 54, 1946, pp. 375-388, illus., diagrs., drgs., graph data. Aerojet's JATO motors.

The B.M.W. 003 jet propulsion engine. *Aircraft Engineering*, vol. 18, no. 204 (February 1946), pp. 43-49, 62, illus., diagrs., drgs., graph and tab. data, and one large fold-out drg.

Notes on the Westinghouse jet engine; some particulars of one of the first successful American axial compressor engines. *Aircraft Engineering*, vol. 18, no. 210 (August 1946), pp. 254-258, illus., drgs., diagrs., tab. data.

Lundquist, W. G., and Cole, R. W. BMW-003 turbo-jet engine compared with the Jumo 004. *SAE Transactions*, vol. 54, 1946, pp. 503-510, illus., graph data.

Notes on the Bristol Theseus heat-exchanger propeller turbine. *Aircraft Engineering*, vol. 18, no. 213 (November 1946), pp. 366-371, illus., drgs., diagrs., phantom view, graph and tab. data.

Boxter, A. D. Aircraft rocket motors, with special reference to German developments with hydrogen peroxide. *Aircraft Engineering*, vol. 19, no. 222 (August 1947), pp. 249-257, illus., diagrs., graph data.

Maguire, D. R. Enemy jet history. *Journal of the Royal Aeronautical Society* (January 1948), vol. 52, pp. 75-84, illus., drgs., diagrs., bibl.

The development of turbine engines in France. *Aircraft Engineering*, vol. 21, no. 246 (August 1949), pp. 244-247; no. 247 (September 1949), pp. 293-296; and no. 248 (October 1949), pp. 328-330. Illus., drgs., diagrs., graph data.

Proteus and coupled-Proteus turbines. *The Aeroplane*, vol. 77, no. 2009 (December 9, 1949), pp. 783–787, illus., diagrs., graph data, and phantom view drg.

Jet controversy. *Interavia*, vol. 7, no. 9, 1952, pp. 502–503. Whittle and Heinkel.

DRIGGS, I. H., and LANCASTER, O. E. Gas turbine development: Aviation. ASME, *Transactions*, vol. 75 (1953), pp. 217–234, illus., diagrs., graph and tab. data, bibl. of 10 items.

TAYLOR, P. B. The first 100 years of aircraft powerplants. *SAE Journal*, vol. 63, no. 2 (February 1955), pp. 89–92. Past and future "history" to the year 2005. Includes material on early jet engines.

MARTIN, JAMES A. The record-setting research airplanes. *Aerospace Engineering*, vol. 21, no. 12 (December 1962), pp. 49–54, illus., tab. and graph data, bibl. From Bell X–1 to North American X–15, including data on their engines.

ELTIS, E. M., and MORLEY, F. W. The engine's contribution to economic short-haul jet transport. *SAE Transactions*, vol. 73, 1965, pp. 609–620, illus. chart, graph and tab. data.

See also under History and Technology (DRIGGS and LANCASTER, 1955; GODDARD and PENDRAY, 1961; LEY, 1961; PRATT, 1965; SMITH, 1942). And under NACA Reports, *9th, 1923* (BUCKINGHAM).

Related Technical Developments

For articles containing information on engine vibration and its control see under History and Technology (HOLZER, 1921). Also under Aircraft Powerplants, *Engines 1925–1929* (CARTER, 1927). *Engines 1935–1939* (LÜRENBAUM, 1936; TAYLOR, 1936; DRAPER, 1938; HAZEN and MONTIETH, 1938; TAYLOR and BROWNE, 1938; BENTLEY, 1939; BROWNE, 1939). *Piston Engines 1940 and after* (CARTER and FORSHAW, 1943).

For articles containing information on valves see under Aircraft Powerplants, *Engines 1920–1924* (HERON, 1922). *Engines 1935–1939* ("The Coming of the Sleeve Valve" 1937; How the Sleeve Valve Works," 1937; FEDDEN, 1938). *Piston Engines 1940 and After* (COLWELL, 1940, "The Development of Sodium Cooling of Exhaust Valves," 1940).

Altitude Performance and Supercharging

American engine tests under high altitude conditions. *The Aeroplane*, vol. 17, August 27, 1919, pp. 835–838, and September 3, 1919, pp. 921–924. Graph data.

HALLETT, E. A. Superchargers and supercharging engines. *SAE Journal*, vol. 5, no. 5 (November 1919), pp. 371–375. Sherbondy (1918) with the U.S. Rateau-Bateau Smoot Co.; three examples built (1919); poor cooling. G.E. machine tested at Pike's Peak (1918); new G.E. type under test in flight (1919).

GAGE, V. R. Some factors of engine performance. *SAE Transactions*, vol. 15, pt. 1, 1920, pp. 963–982. Analysis of Bureau of Standards altitude chamber tests.

SPARROW, S. W. Flying an airplane engine on the ground. *SAE Transactions*, vol. 15, pt. 1, 1920, pp. 608–624. Considerable graph data; relates to laboratory and test stand work.

DEBOTHEZAT, GEORGE. Airplane performance as influenced by the supercharged engine. *NACA Technical Note*, no. 2, 1920, 7 pp.

Devillers, René. The problem of the turbo-compressor. *NACA Technical Note*, no. 11, 1920, 28 pp.

Schwager, Otto. Notes on the design of supercharged and over-dimensioned aircraft motors. Transl. from *Technische Berichte*, vol. 3. *NACA Technical Note*, no. 7, 1920, 6 pp.

McCready, John A. Functioning of supercharger in altitude flight. *Aviation*, vol. 12, no. 2 (January 9, 1922), p. 51. McCready, as pilot of the LePere airplane with a turbo-supercharged Liberty engine made the world's high-altitude record in 1921.

Gregg, David. Superchargers. *Aviation*, vol. 19, no. 4 (July 27, 1925), pp. 90–92, illus., drgs.

Gardner, Arthur W. A Roots-type engine supercharger. *SAE Transactions*, vol. 21, pt. 2 (1926), pp. 911–943, illus., drgs., graph data.

Short, C. R. Supercharging internal-combustion engines. *SAE Transactions*, vol. 21, pt. 1, 1926, pp. 235–274, illus., drgs. History as of 1925. First G.E. model, May 1918, on Liberty engine; first flight, spring of 1919.

Fedden, A. H. R. The supercharging of aircraft and motor-vehicle engines. *Journal of the Royal Aeronautical Society* (September 1927), vol. 31, pp. 933–972, illus., drgs., diagrs., graph data.

Korvin-Kroukovsky, B. V. The high altitude airplane; engineering problems in the design of an airplane to navigate in the stratosphere. *Aviation*, vol. 26, no. 16 (April 20, 1929), Aeronautical Engineering Section, pp. liv–lxi; and no. 20 (May 18, 1929), pp. lxxviii–lxxxiv.

Roots supercharger on Soucek plane proves efficiency of blower type. *Automotive Industries*, vol. 60, no. 24 (June 15, 1929), pp. 911–913, illus. Comments on the 1929 world's altitude record with this equipment.

Johnston, S. Paul. The present status of aircraft engine superchargers. *Aviation*, vol. 29, no. 6 (December 1930), pp. 358–359.

Berger, A. L., and Chenoweth, Opie. The turbo supercharger. *SAE Transactions*, vol. 26, 1931, pp. 592–607, illus., graph data. Emphasis is historical.

Schey, Oscar W. Superchargers and supercharging. *SAE Transactions*, vol. 26, 1931, pp. 581–591, illus., graph data.

Cummings, H. K., and Garlock, E. A. Altitude laboratory tests of aircraft engines. ASME, *Transactions*, vol. 54, 1932, pp. 53–60, illus.

Ragazzi, Paolo. The power of aircraft engines at altitude. *NACA Technical Memorandum*, no. 895, 1939, 38 pp., illus., diagrs., graph and tab. data, bibl. of 5 items.

Gasterstädt, J. Junkers diesel motors and supercharging. *The Aeroplane*, vol. 42, no. 1342 (February 10, 1937), pp. 165–169, illus., drgs., graph data. A Lilienthal Gesellschaft lecture. German application of the turbo-supercharger.

Sarracino, Marcello. New method of calculating the power at altitude of aircraft engines equipped with superchargers on the basis of tests made under sea-level conditions. *NACA Technical Memorandum*, no. 981, 1941, 32 pp., graph data, bibl. of 6 items.

Kendrick, James B. Ground versus flight tests of airplane engine installations. *SAE Transactions*, vol. 50, 1942, pp. 241–251, illus., diagrs., graph data, and a 7-item bibliography.

Above the dark blue weather; airplanes that are to fly in the stratosphere. *Aviation*, vol. 31, no. 5 (May 1932), pp. 225–226, illus., drgs.

DROEGMULLER, E. A., and HERSEY, D. S. The relation of intake-charge cooling to engine performance. *SAE Transactions*, vol. 52, 1944, pp. 614–620, graph data.

CAMPBELL, KENNETH, and TALBERT, JOHN E. Some advantages and limitations of centrifugal and axial aircraft superchargers. *SAE Transactions*, vol. 53, 1945, pp. 607–618, illus., graph data.

A pioneer passes. *The Aeroplane* (November 22, 1946), vol. 71, p. 611. Obituary, Dr. Sanford Moss.

Also see articles in the following NACA Reports: *1st, 1915; 3d, 1917; 4th, 1918; 6th, 1920; 11th, 1925; 13th, 1927; 14th, 1928; 16th, 1930; 17th, 1931.*

Cooling, Cowling, and Radiators

BLACK, ARCHIBALD. Aircraft radiators. *SAE Transactions*, vol. 14, pt. 1, 1919, pp. 534–577. Complete and well documented, from early Wright machine to date; includes a 43-item bibl.

PARSONS, SAMUEL R. Design factors for airplane radiators. *SAE Transactions*, vol. 15, pt. 1, 1920, pp. 591–608.

The Lamblin Radiator. *The Aeroplane* (January 19, 1921), vol. 20, p. 66, illus.

Clark plane and Low-Drag Cowl. *Aviation*, vol. 26, no. 12 (March 23, 1929), p. 898. Anticipation of NACA cowling in 1921.

WEICK, FRED E. The new NACA low drag cowling. *Aviation*, vol. 25, no. 21 (November 17, 1928), pp. 1556–1557, 1586, 1588, 1590, illus.

BRIDGMAN, LEONARD, and JAMES, THURSTAN. The cowling of air-cooled engines. *The Aeroplane* (January 30, 1929), vol. 36, pp. 160A–164A, illus.

ANGLE, GLENN D. Radial vs. in-line engines. ASME, *Transactions*, vol. 51, 1929, pp. 189–196. Part of the air- versus liquid-cooling controversy.

FRANK, G. W. High temperature liquid cooling. *SAE Transactions*, vol. 24, 1929, pp. 445–459. illus., graph data. Relates to use of engine coolants other than water.

More about the cowling of air-cooled engines. *The Aeroplane* (April 24, 1929), vol. 36, pp. 653–654, 656, illus.

SWAN, ANDREW. Recent developments in cooling aero-engines. *Journal of the Royal Aeronautical Society* (March 1931), vol. 35, pp. 179–206. Summarized in *The Aeroplane* (November 26, 1930), vol. 34, pp. 1240–1244.

TOWNEND, H. C. H. The Townend ring. *Journal of the Royal Aeronautical Society* (October 1930), vol. 34, pp. 813–848, illus., drgs., diagrs., graph data.

BOYD, PAUL M. Engine cowl rings. ASME, *Transactions*, vol. 54, 1932, pp. 93–101. Historical point of view.

HIGGINBOTHAM, R. R. Engine cooling problems with venturi cowling. *SAE, Transactions*, vol. 27, 1932, 84–92, illus., diagrs., tab. data. Cowling of radial engines; experince of Stearman Aircraft Co.

BEISEL, REX B., MACCLAIN, A. L., and THOMAS, F. M. The cowling and cooling of radial engines. *Journal of the Royal Aeronautical Society* (July 1934), vol. 38, pp. 613–650, illus., diagrs., graph data. Orginally given as a paper before ASME 1934 annual meeting.

KEMPER, C. Fin and baffle design for air-cooled engines. *SAE Transactions*, vol. 29, 1934, pp. 370–376. Summary of work by NACA.

NORTH, J. D. Engine cowling. *Journal of the Royal Aeronautical Society* (July 1934), vol. 38, pp. 566–612, illus., diagrs., graph data. Broad historical treatment.

SHOEMAKER, J. M., RHINES, T. B., and SARGENT, H. H., JR. Further progress in controlled cooling of radial engines. *SAE Transactions*, vol. 30, 1935, pp. 349–360, illus., diagrs., graph data. Relates to cowl flaps.

Ducted radiators for aero-engines. *Interavia*, no. 357 (September 3, 1936), pp. 1–3.

ANDERSON, P. A. Air-cooled radial aircraft engine installation. *SAE Transactions*, vol. 31, 1936, pp. 341–350, illus., drgs., diagrs.

WOOD, DONALD H. Engine nacelles and propellers and airplane performance. *SAE Transactions*, vol. 38, 1936, pp. 148–160, illus., drgs., diagrs., tab. and graph data.

BEISEL, REX B. Why use cowl flaps? *Journal of the Aeronautical Sciences*, vol. 4, no. 5 (May 1937), pp. 185–191, illus.

CAMPBELL, KENNETH. Cylinder cooling and drag of radial engine installations. *SAE Transactions*, vol. 33, 1938, pp. 515–528, illus., drgs., graph data. Relates to cowlings, cowl flaps, and baffle designs.

LEE, JOHN G. Air-cooled vs. liquid-cooled aircraft. *Journal of the Aeronautical Sciences*, vol. 8, no. 6 (April 1941), pp. 219–229, illus., diagrs., graph data.

RICKERT, P., and HELD, A. Heat transfer in geometrically similar cylinders. *NACA Technical Memorandum*, no. 977, 1941, 11 pp., graph data, bibl. of 3 items.

Also see articles in the following NACA Reports: *4th, 1918; 5th, 1919; 6th, 1920; 13th, 1927; 15th, 1929; 21st, 1935; 23rd, 1937; 24th, 1938; 25th, 1939.*

Carburetors, Carburetion, and Fuel Injection

Development of Stromberg carburetors. *Aviation*, vol. 23, no. 5 (August 1, 1927), p. 247.

WILLGOOS, A. V. D. Pratt and Whitney fuel injection system. *U.S. Air Services*, vol. 17, No. 2 (February 1932), pp. 35–36.

CLOTHIER, W. C. Ice formation in carburetors. *Journal of the Royal Aeronautical Society* (September 1935), vol. 39, pp. 761–806, diagrs., graph data.

Pratt & Whitney automatic power and mixture control. *Aero Digest*, vol. 26, no. 1 (July 1935), pp. 38–40, 42.

Automatic mixture: New Pratt & Whitney carburetor control gets long workout on first Pan American flight. *Aviation*, vol. 34, no. 6 (June 1935), pp. 35–36.

BEARDSLEY, GUY E. An automatic power and mixture control for aircraft engines. *SAE Transactions*, vol. 37, 1935, pp. 301–306, illus., diagrs., graph data.

Automatic power and mixture control. *The Aeroplane*, vol. 52 (May 5, 1937), pp. 540–541, diagrs.

KITTLER, M. J. A non-icing fully maneuverable aircraft carburetor. *SAE Transactions*, vol. 34, 1939, pp. 357–364, illus., graph data.

The Stromberg injection type aircraft carburetor. *Automotive Industries*, vol. 84, no. 12 (June 15, 1941), pp. 620–624.

Three German engine fuel systems. *Aircraft Engineering*, vol. 15, no. 175 (September 1943), pp. 248–253, and no. 176 (October 1943), pp. 293–302. Brilliantly illustrated. These fuel-injection systems are from the BMW 132, the Bramo-Fafnir 323P, and the BMW 801.

WEIGAND, F. J. Carburetion for the aircraft engine. *SAE Transactions*, vol. 51 (1943), pp. 294–303, illus., drgs., diagrs., graph data.

THORNER, ROBERT H. *Aircraft carburetion.* New York: John Wiley, 1946. 393 pp., illus., diagrs. The book is an outgrowth of a series of lectures given at the University of Michigan during 1942.

LANGE, GEORGE M. Fuel injection for low-horsepower aircraft engines. *SAE Journal* (April 1947), vol. 55, pp. 48–52, illus., drgs.

REID, R. A. S. Aero-engine injection carburetors. *Aircraft Engineering*, vol. 19, no. 216 (February 1947), pp. 38–42, diagrs. and phantom view.

Improved fuel-injection system for Mercedes-Benz engine. *Automotive Industries*, vol. 119, no. 8 (October 15, 1958), p. 63, illus., diagrs.

WISEMAN, William A. Continental's fuel injection for business aircraft. *Automotive Industries*, vol. 118, no. 8 (April 15, 1958), pp. 55–60, 154–155, diagrs.

Also see articles in the following NACA Reports: *2d, 1916; 4th, 1920; 19th, 1933.*

Instruments and Accessories

MACHOL, MORRIS R. Spark gaps in series with spark plugs. *Aviation*, vol. 2, no. 11 (July 1, 1917), p. 498. Condensation of a paper given at 10th annual convention of the National Gas Engine Assn., June 7, 1917.

BLACK, ARCHIBALD. Exhaust headers and mufflers for airplane engines. *SAE Transactions*, vol. 13, pt. 2, 1918, pp. 292–306, illus., drgs., bibl.

HEALD, R. H. Performance of a vane-driven gear pump. *NACA Technical Note*, no. 61, 1921, 20 pp., diagrs., graph data.

The aeromarine starter. *Aviation*, vol. 19, no. 13 (September 28, 1925), pp. 391–392. First inertia type.

The Heywood injector starter. *Aviation*, vol. 23, no. 24 (December 12, 1927), pp. 1408–1409. A combined air and gasoline type.

ROBERTSON, E. A., and HULL, L. M. Suppressing ignition-interference on radio-equipped aircraft. *SAE Transactions*, vol. 25, 1930, pp. 260–266, illus., diagrs.

History of the scintilla magneto. *Aviation Engineering*, vol. 8, no. 1 (January 1933), p. 27.

STUNKEL, REAGAN C. Aircraft accessories: Spark plugs. *Southwestern Aviation*, vol. 2, no. 3 (September 1934), pp. 14–15.

BOYNTON, H. G. Autosyn remote indicating system. *Aero Digest*, vol. 28, no. 5 (May 1936), pp. 48, 50. Remote-reading instruments for engines in very large aircraft.

GRAY, HAROLD E. Radio shielding on air transports. *SAE Transactions*, vol. 32, 1937, pp. 527–530. At this date Gray was a captain with Pan American Airways; later became president of the organization.

Hydraulic starter for aircraft engine. *Automotive Industries*, vol. 76, no. 17 (April 24, 1937), p. 622, illus., diagr.

CRONSTEDT, VAL. Shortcomings of mica insulation for aviation spark plugs. *SAE Journal*, vol. 46, no. 6 (June 1940), pp. 233–235.

RIDDLE, FRANK H. Ceramic insulators for spark plugs. *SAE Journal*, vol. 46, no. 6 (June 1940), pp. 236–242.

HOLLIDAY, T. B., LT. COL., USAAF. Aircraft accessory systems. *SAE Transactions*, vol. 51, 1943, pp. 234–240, 247, illus., diagrs., graph data.

Spark plugs for internal-combustion engines. *Lubrication*, vol. 35, no. 6 (June 1949), pp. 61–72, illus., drgs. Traces some historical development.

Also see articles in the following NACA Reports: *2d, 1916; 5th, 1919; 7th, 1921; 10th, 1924; 12th, 1926; 16th, 1930; 19th, 1933.*

Fuels and Combustion, Lubrication

KETTERING, CHARLES F. More efficient utilization of fuel. *SAE Transactions*, vol. 14, pt. 1, 1919, pp. 201–219. Discussion of engine "knocking" and its relation to fuel structure; indicator cards from optical indicator. Cyclohexane did not knock in Liberty cylinder with 200-lb compression; "best" gasoline 125 lb.

MIDGLEY, THOMAS, JR. The combustion of fuels in the internal-combustion engine. *SAE Transactions*, vol. 15, pt. 2, 1920, pp. 659–696. Discussion of fuel structure and its relation to engine behavior; optical indicator shows pressure waves due to detonation; theory of "knock"; mentions iodine and analin as knock suppressors.

KUTZBACH, K. The problem of fuel for aviation engines. *NACA Technical Note*, no. 62, 1921, 22 pp., graph and tab. data. A lecture given at the Aldershof Aero Lab., Germany.

WYMAN, W. W. Effect of low grade gasoline on engines. *Aviation*, vol. 11, no. 20 (November 14, 1921), pp. 575–576.

CAUTLEY, R. B. Fuel and oil consumption important factors in long distance flights; good results obtained by Charles A. Lindbergh with a Whirlwind air-cooled engine. *Aviation*, vol. 22, no. 23 (June 6, 1927), pp. 1214–1215, 1243.

JONES, E. T. Fuel for the Wright "Whirlwind." *Aviation*, vol. 23, no. 20 (November 14, 1927), pp. 1170–1172.

STALEY, F. R. Some pertinent facts about aviation engine oils. *Aviation*, vol. 27, no. 6 (August 10, 1929), pp. 304–305, illus.

CUMMINGS, H. K. Gasoline requirements of commercial aircraft engines. *SAE Transactions*, vol. 25, 1930, pp. 161–163.

DOOLITTLE, JAMES H. Volatility requirements of aircraft fuels. *SAE Transactions*, vol. 25, 1930, pp. 170–172.

HERON, S. D. Fuel requirements of the gasoline aircraft engine. *SAE Transactions*, vol. 25, 1930, pp. 164–169.

———. High performance gasoline aircraft engine: Its problems of fuel, oil, and materials of cylinder construction. *ASME, Transactions*, vol. 52 (1930), pp. 233–253.

NEVILLE, LESLIE E. The S.A.E. discusses fuel. *Aviation*, vol. 29, no. 5 (November 1930), pp. 273–277, diagrs., tab. data.

BANKS, F. R. Fuels for aircraft engines *Journal of the Royal Aeronautical Society* (February 1932), vol. 36, pp. 127–140, graph data.

WARD, B. P., and SINCLAIR, W. P. Testing of naval aviation gasoline. *Journal of the American Society of Naval Engineers*, vol. 44, no. 3 (August 1932), pp. 285–297.

What is an octane number? *The Aeroplane* (March 9, 1932), vol. 42, pp. 436–437.

BANKS, F. R. Ethyl: Some information on the use and advantages gained by the Employment of tetraethyl lead in fuels for aviation engines. *Journal of the Royal Aeronautical Society* (April 1934), vol. 38, pp. 309–372, graph data.

KLEIN, F. D. Aircraft engine performance with 100 octane fuel. *Journal of the American Institute of Aeronautical Sciences* (March 1935), vol. 2, pp. 43–47.

NUTT, ARTHUR. Aircraft engines and their lubrication. *SAE Transactions*, vol. 34, 1939, pp. 501–512, illus., drgs., diagrs.

Synthetic oils for aircraft gas turbine lubrication. *Lubrication*, vol. 40, no. 4 (April 1954), pp. 45–56, illus., diagrs., schematic views.

Also see articles in the following NACA Reports: *11th, 1925; 13th, 1927; 15th, 1929; 20th, 1934; 21st, 1935; 24th, 1938; 25th, 1939.*

Propellers and Propeller Gearing

PILLET, L. Expériences practiques sur le rendiment de différentes hélices aérienne. *L'Aéronaute*, vol. 3, no. 3 (March 1870), pp. 33–43, tabular data.

FROUDE, W. On the Elementary Relation Between Pitch, Slip, and Propulsive Efficiency. *Transactions*, Institution of Naval Architects [British], vol. 19, 1878, pp. 47–65.

ARSON, —. Etude sur le Propulseur pour l'Aviation. Société des Ingénieurs Civils de France, *Mémoires*, vol. 32, 1879, pp. 342–365.

AMANS, P. C. Perfectionnement des hélices aériennes. *L'Aéronaute*, vol. 25, no. 10 (October 1892), pp. 219–231, diagrs.

CALDWELL, F. W. Conventional propeller calculations. *SAE Transactions*, vol. 13, pt. 2, 1918, pp. 307–333, illus., drgs., diagrs., graph data.

EIFFEL, GUSTAVE. *Études sur l'hélice aérienne faites au laboratoire d'Aureil; les nouvelles recherches sur les hélices aérienne.* Paris: E. Chiron, 1921. 304 pp., illus.

Description of the Curtiss-Reed metal propeller. *Aviation*, vol. 15, no. 21 (November 19, 1923), p. 630.

The Paragon adjustable and reversible propeller. *Aviation*, vol. 14, no. 1 (January 1, 1923), p. 19.

The Leitner-Watts metal propeller; uses hollow steel blades set in adjustable hub. *Aviation*, vol. 19, no. 9 (August 31, 1925), pp. 244–245, illus.

WRIGHT, THEODORE P. The durability of metal propellers. *Aviation*, vol. 21, no. 17 (October 25, 1926), p. 706; no. 22 (November 29, 1926), pp. 913–914; and no. 26 (December 27, 1926), pp. 1082–1083.

MCCAULEY, E. G. Metal propeller development; extensive test work responsible for present efficiency. *Aviation*, vol. 22, no. 22 (May 30, 1927), pp. 1127–1130, 1444, illus.

MOCK, RICHARD M. Geared down propellers and the efficiency of commercial airplanes. *Aviation*, vol. 22, no. 22 (May 30, 1927), pp. 1137–1140, illus., graphs and tab. data.

HAVILL, CLINTON H., LCDR., USN. Development of aircraft propellers. *Aviation*, vol. 25, no. 16 (October 13, 1928), pp. 1190, 1206–1208. An excellent survey.

Success of new variable pitch propeller indicated by British company's experiments. *Aviation*, vol. 24, no. 26 (June 25, 1928), p. 1856. Gloster's Dr. Hele-Shaw and T. E. Beacham.

The Turnbull variable pitch propeller. *Aviation*, vol. 24, no. 8 (February 20, 1928), pp 446–448, illus.

HELE-SHAW, H. S., and BEACHAM, T. E. The variable pitch airscrew. *Journal of the Royal Aeronautical Society* (July 1928), vol. 32, pp. 525–554, illus., drgs., diagrs.

CALDWELL, FRANK W. Variable pitch propellers. *SAE Transactions*, vol. 24 (1929), pp. 467–477, drgs., diagrs., graph data. Caldwell was chief engineer of the Standard Propeller Co.

WRIGHT, THEODORE P., and TURNBULL, W. R. Controllable pitch propeller. *SAE Transactions*, vol. 24, 1929, pp. 478–485, 497, graph data.

———, and JOHNSON, R. E. Gearing of aircraft propellers. *SAE Transactions*, vol. 24, 1929, pp. 486–491.

WARNER, EDWARD P. The S.A.E. propeller and power plant sessions. *Aviation*, vol. 27, no. 9 (August 31, 1929), pp. 469–473, illus.

DICKY, D. A., and COOK, O. R. Controllable and automatic aircraft propellers. *SAE Transactions*, vol. 27, 1932, pp. 105–111, illus. Descriptions of early types.

CHATFIELD, CHARLES HUGH. Controllable pitch propellers in transport service. *Aviation*, vol. 32, no. 6 (June 1933), pp. 180–181.

Effect of controllable pitch on airplane performance. *Aviation Engineering*, vol. 8, no. 3 (March 1933), pp. 14–15, 25, illus., diagrs.

LOMBARD, A. E., and WRIGHT, THEODORE P. Pitch control. *Aviation*, vol. 32, no 12 (December 1933), pp. 376–378, illus., graphs, and tab. data.

CALDWELL, F. W. Aircraft propeller development and testing summarized. *SAE Transactions*, vol. 29, 1934, pp. 297–303 (part 2) and 349–354 (part 2).

CARROLL, GEORGE. Not too technical: The function of propellers. *Southwestern Aviation*, vol. 2, no. 4 (October 1934), pp. 21–22, and no. 5 (November 1934), pp. 17, 29. Diagrs.

Operating principles of the constant speed propeller. *Aero Digest*, vol. 29, no. 3 (September 1936), pp. 36–37, 84, illus.

Propeller governor. *Aviation*, vol. 35, no. 9 (September 1936), pp. 36–37, illus. Hamilton-Standard constant speed model.

CALDWELL, F. W., MARTIN, E., and RHINES, T. B. The constant speed propeller: Performance and control. *SAE Transactions*, vol. 32, 1937, pp. 28–44, illus., drgs., diagrs., graph data.

Curtiss controllable: An electric constant speed, full-feathering propeller. *Aviation*, vol. 36, no. 5 (May 1937), pp. 38–39, 73, illus.

Curtiss electric constant speed propeller. *Aero Digest*, vol. 30, no. 5 (May 1937), pp. 48, 50, illus.

A fully feathering airscrew; details of the Curtiss-Wright 120-degree angular range electrical operation. *Flight*, vol. 14, no. 5 (May 27, 1937), Engineering Supplement, pp. 29–31, illus.

JABLONSKY, BRUNO. Airscrews at the Paris aero show. *The Aeroplane*, vol. 52 (February 3, 1937), pp. 139–141, and vol. 52 (February 17, 1937), pp. 193–195, illus., diagrs.

BAKER, CARL F. Propeller problems imposed by substratosphere flight. *SAE Transactions*, vol. 33, 1938, pp. 285–288, 300.

LAMPTON, G. T. Propeller factors tending to limit aircraft engine powers. *SAE Transactions*, vol. 33, 1938, pp. 289–292, graph data.

MCSURELY, ALEXANDER. The Wrights and the propeller. *The Bee Hive*, vol. 28, no. 2 (Spring 1953), pp. 20–24, illus.

MOLSON, K. M. Some historial notes on the development of the variable pitch propeller. *Canadian Aeronautics and Space Journal* (June 1965), vol. 11, pp. 177–183, illus., bibliography of 25 items.

National Advisory Committee for Aeronautics

Annual Reports, 1915–1939

1st Annual Report, 1915

MARVIN, CHARLES F. Preliminary report on the problem of the atmosphere in relation to aeronautics. Report 4 in *First Annual Report of the National Advisory Committee for Aeronautics, 1915* (Washington: Government Printing Office, 1916),* pp. 129–130.

LUCKE, CHARLES E. Thermodynamic efficiency of present types of internal combustion engines for aircraft: Part I, Review of the development of engines suitable for Aeronautic service; Part II, Aero engines analyzed with reference to elements of Process or function. Report 7 in NACA, *1st Annual Report, 1915* (1916), pp. 186–303. Extensive tab. data. An excellent source of information about engines of that time.

2d Annual Report, 1916

General specifications covering requirements of aeronautic instruments. Report 8 in NACA, *2d Annual Report, 1916* (1917), pp. 25–28.

Nomenclature for aeronautics. Report 9 in NACA, *2d Annual Report, 1916* (1917), pp. 31–37.

DIEDERICHS, H., and UPTON, G. B., Mufflers for aeronautic engines. Report 10 in NACA, *2d Annual Report*, 1916 (1917), pp. 41–49, drgs., tab. data. In spite of such work, mufflers have seldom been used on aircraft engines.

LUCKE, CHARLES EDWARD, and WILLHÖFFT, FRIEDRICH OTTO. Carburetor design—a preliminary study of the state of the art. Report 11 in NACA, *2d Annual Report, 1916* (1917), pp. 53–552. Structured in seven chapters, this report is profusely illustrated with drgs. from patents, accompanied by extensive discussions. An outstanding source of information on carburetor design in 1916.

3d Annual Report, 1917

DICKINSON, H. C. Aeronautic power plant investigations: 1. Performance of aeronautic engines at high altitudes; 2, Radiator design; 3, Spark plugs. Report 23 in NACA, *3d Annual Report, 1917* (1918), pp. 479–495, drgs., diagrs.

4th Annual Report, 1918

PARIS, AUGUST JEAN, JR., and PARIS, W. FRANCKLYN. A new process for the production of aircraft engine fuels. Report 42 in NACA, *4th Annual Report* (1918), pp. 473–476. Graph data.

DICKINSON, H. C., and KLEINSCHMIDT, R. V. Synopsis of Aeronautic Radiator Investigations for Years 1917 and 1918. Report 43 in NACA, *4th Annual Report, 1918* (1920), pp. 477–482.

———, and BOUTELL, H. G. The altitude laboratory for the testing of aircraft engines. Report 44 in NACA, *4th Annual Report, 1918* (1920), pp. 483–498, drgs., diagrs.

———, JAMES, W. S., and ANDERSON, G. V. Effect of compression ratio, pressure, temperature, and humidity on power. Report 45 in NACA, *4th Annual Report, 1918* (1920), pp. 499–524, graph data.

---

*Hereafter, title abbreviated as in next entry.

GAGE, VICTOR R. A study of airplane engine tests. Report 46 in NACA, *4th Annual Report, 1918* (1920), pp. 525–559, extensive graph and tab. data.

DICKINSON, H. C., and others. Power characteristics of fuels for aircraft engines. Report 47, pts. 1, 2, and 3, in NACA, *4th Annual Report*, 1918 (1920), pp. 560–589, graph and tab. data.

TICE, PERCIVAL S. Carbureting conditions characteristic of aircraft engines. Report 48 in NACA, *4th Annual Report, 1918* (1920), pp. 590–595.

———. Metering characteristics of carburetors. Report 49, in NACA, *4th Annual Report, 1918* (1920), pp. 596–643, drgs., diagrs., graph and tab. data.

KEMBLE, E. C. Calculation of low-pressure indicator diagrams. Report 50, in NACA, *4th Annual Report, 1918* (1920), pp. 644–654, graph data.

5th Annual Report, 1919

SILSBEE, F. B. Causes of failure of spark plugs. Report 51, pt. 1, in NACA, *5th Annual Report, 1919* (1920), pp. 43–52, illus.

LOEB, L. B., SAWYER. L. G., and FONESCA, E. L. Gas leakage in spark plugs. Report 51, pt. 2, in NACA, *5th Annual Report, 1919* (1920), pp. 53–62, diagr., graph and tab. data.

DICKINSON, H. C., SILSBEE, F. B., and AGNEW, A. G. Methods for testing spark plugs. Report 51, pt. 3, in NACA, *5th Annual Report, 1919* (1920), pp. 63–70, diagrs.

CRAGOE, C. S. Temperatures in spark plugs having steel and brass shells. Report 52 in NACA, *5th Annual Report, 1919* (1920), pp. 73–76, diagrs., graph data.

SILSBEE, F. B., and others. Properties and preparation of ceramic insulators for spark plugs. Report 53, pts. 1–4, in NACA, *5th Annual Report, 1919* (1920), pp. 79–111, drgs., diagrs., graph and tab. data.

LOEB, L. B., and SILSBEE, F. B. Effect of temperature and pressure on the sparking voltage. Report 54 in NACA, *5th Annual Report, 1919* (1920), pp. 115–121, diagrs., graph data.

UPTON, G. B., and GAGE, V. R. Investigation of the muffling problem for airplane engines. Report 55 in NACA, *5th Annual Report, 1919* (1920), pp. 125–160, illus., drgs., graph and tab. data.

SILSBEE, F. B., LOEB, L. B., and FONESCA, E. L. Method of measuring heat energy of ignition sparks. Report 56 in NACA, *5th Annual Report, 1919* (1920), pp. 163–176, diagrs., graph data.

GORTON, W. S. The subsidiary gap as a means for improving ignition. Report 57 in NACA, *5th Annual Report, 1919* (1920), pp. 179–190.

SILSBEE, F. B. Characteristics of high-tension magnetos. Report 58 in NACA, *5th Annual Report, 1919* (1920), pp. 193–213, diagrs., graph data.

DICKINSON, H. C., JAMES, W. S., and KLEINSCHMIDT, R. V. General analysis of airplane radiator problems. Report 59 in NACA, *5th Annual Report, 1919* (1920), pp. 217–221.

———, JAMES, W. S., and BROWN, W. B. General discussion of test methods for radiators. Report 60 in NACA, *5th Annual Report, 1919* (1920), pp. 225–244, diagrs, tab. data.

KLEINSCHMIDT, R. B., and PARSONS, S. R. Head resistance due to radiators. Report 61 in NACA, *5th Annual Report, 1919* (1920), pp. 247–264, graph data.

JAMES, W. S., and PARSONS, S. R. Effect of altitude on radiator performance. Report 62 in NACA, *5th Annual Report, 1919* (1920), pp. 267–275, graph data.

DICKINSON, H. C., JAMES, W. C., and KLEINSCHMIDT, R. V. Results of tests on radiators for aircraft engines. Report 63 in NACA, *5th Annual Report, 1919* (1920), pp. 279-316, illus., drgs., tab. data.

6th Annual Report, 1920

PARSONS, S. R. Properties of special types of radiators. Report 86 in NACA, *6th Annual Report, 1920* (1921), pp. 133-147, illus., graph and tab. data.

———, and KLEINSCHMIDT, R. V. Effects of nature of cooling surface on radiator performance. Report 87 in NACA, *6th Annual Report, 1920* (1921), pp. 151-159, graph data.

———. Pressure drop in radiator air tubes. Report 88 in NACA, *6th Annual Report, 1920* (1921), pp. 163-169, graph and tab. data.

GAGE, VICTOR R., SPARROW, STANWOOD W., and HARPER, D. R. Comparison of AlcoGas aviation fuel with export aviation gasoline. Report 89 in NACA, *6th Annual Report, 1920* (1921), pp 173-184, extensive graph data.

DICKINSON, H. C., GAGE, Victor R., and SPARROW, STANWOOD W. Comparison of hecter fuel with export aviation gasoline. Report 90 in NACA, *6th Annual Report, 1920* (1921), pp. 187-194, graph data.

SPARROW, STANWOOD W., and WHITE, H. S. Performance of a Liberty 12 airplane engine. Report 102 in NACA, *6th Annual Report, 1920* (1921), pp. 561-578, extensive graph and tab. data on tests in the Bureau of Standards altitude chamber, the first facility of its kind.

———, and WHITE, H. S. Performance of a 300-horsepower Hispano-Suiza airplane engine. Report 103 in NACA, *6th Annual Report, 1920* (1921), pp. 581-600, extensive graph and tab. data. Tests in Bureau of Standards altitude chamber.

PARSONS, S. R. Turbulence in the air tubes of radiators for aircraft engines. Report 106 in NACA, *6th Annual Report, 1920* (1921), pp. 623-633, diagrs., graph and tab. data.

DICKINSON, H. C., and NEWELL, F. B. A high-speed engine pressure indicator of the balanced diaphragm type. Report 107 in NACA, *6th Annual Report, 1920* (1921), pp. 637-648, illus., drgs. diagrs., graph and tab. data. The development of the indicator by the Bureau of Standards was an important contribution to the future development of aircraft engines.

GAGE, Victor R. Some factors of airplane engine performance. Report 108 in NACA, *6th Annual Report, 1920* (1921), pp 651-677, extensive graph and tab. data.

7th Annual Report, 1921

SILSBEE, F. B. Simplified theory of the magneto. Report 123 in NACA, *7th Annual Report, 1921* (1923), pp. 405-419, diagrs., graph data.

WASHBURN, G. E., SYLVANDER, R. C., MUELLER, E. F., WILHELM, R. M., EATON, H. N., and WARNER, John A. C. Power plant instruments. Report 129 in NACA, *7th Annual Report, 1921* (1923), pp. 667-637, illus., drgs., diagrs., graph and tab. data; includes "keyed" photographs. A very informative item.

8th Annual Report, 1922

SPARROW, STANWOOD W. Performance of Maybach 300-horsepower airplane engine. Report 132 in NACA, *8th Annual Report, 1922* (1923), pp. 91-99, graph data. Sea-level and altitude tests.

———. Performance of B.M.W. 185-horsepower airplane engine. Report 135 in NACA, *8th Annual Report*, *1922* (1923), pp. 103–110, graph data. Sea-level and altitude tests.

HARPER, D. R., and BROWN, W. B. Mathematical equations for heat conduction in the fins of air-cooled engines. Report 158 in NACA, *8th Annual Report*, *1922* (1923), pp. 679–708.

9th Annual Report, 1923

BUCKINGHAM, EDGAR. Jet propulsion for airplanes. Report 159 in NACA, *9th Annual Report*, *1923* (1924), pp. 75–90. Graph and tab. data. It is not very optimistic.

10th Annual Report, 1924

RANDOLPH, D. W., and SILSBEE, F. B. Flame speed and spark intensity. Report 187 in NACA, *10th Annual Report*, *1924* (1925), pp. 81–92, illus., drgs., tab. data.

SPARROW, STANWOOD W. Relation of fuel-air ratio to engine performance. Report 189 in NACA, *10th Annual Report*, *1924* (1925), pp. 109–122, graph data and bibl. of 14 items.

———. Correcting horsepower measurements to standard temperature. Report 190 in NACA, *10th Annual Report*, *1924* (1925), pp. 125–138, graph data and bibl. of 13 items.

SILSBEE, FRANCIS B. The sparking voltage of spark plugs. Report 202 in NACA, *10th Annual Report*, *1924* (1925), pp. 357–370, graph data and bibl. of 71 items.

SPARROW, STANWOOD W. The effect of changes in compression ratio upon engine performance. Report 205 in NACA, *10th Annual Report*, *1924* (1925), pp. 399–518, graph data; bibl. of 12 items.

MILLER, HAROLD E., and BEARDSLEY, EDWARD G. Spray penetration with a simple fuel injection nozzle. Report 222 in NACA, *11th Annual Report*, *1925* (1926), pp. 321–326, diagrs., graph data.

JOACHIM, W. F. An investigation of the coefficient of discharge of liquids through small round orifices. Report 224 in NACA, *11th Annual Report*, *1925* (1926), pp. 371–378, illus., graph data.

11th Annual Report, 1925

WARE, MARSDEN. Description and laboratory tests of a Roots type aircraft engine supercharger. Report 230 in NACA, *11th Annual Report*, *1925* (1926), pp. 451–561, illus., diagrs., graph data.

SPARROW, STANWOOD W. Fuels for high-compression engines. Report 232 in NACA, *11th Annual Report*, *1925* (1926), pp. 483–500, graph data. Partly historical, very descriptive; includes bibl. of 36 items.

12th Annual Report, 1926

PATON, C. R., and KEMPER, CARLTON. Power output and air requirements of a two-stroke cycle engine for aeronautical use. Report 239 in NACA, *12th Annual Report*, *1926* (1927), pp 181–189, graph data, bibl. of 8 items.

BRODE, R. B., RANDOLPH, D. W., and SILSBEE, F. B. Electrical characteristics of spark generators for automotive ignition. Report 241 in NACA, *12th Annual Report*, *1926* (1927), pp. 269–293, graph data, bibl. of 17 items.

GARDINER, ARTHUR W. A preliminary study of fuel injection and compression ignition as applied to an aircraft cylinder. Report 243 in NACA, *12th Annual Report 1926* (1927), pp. 313–326, illus., drgs., diagrs., graph data, bibl. of 4 items.

WARE, MARSDEN. Description of the N.A.C.A. universal test engine and some test results. Report 250 in NACA, *12th Annual Report, 1926* (1927), pp. 469–481, illus., drgs., graph data, bibl. of 4 items. Equipment for single-cylinder research.

GOVE, W. D., and GREEN, M. W. The direct measurement of engine power on an airplane in flight with a hug-type dynamometer. Report 252 in NACA, *12th Annual Report, 1926* (1927), pp. 505–513, illus., drgs., graph data, bibl. of 4 items. Early attempt to measure engine torque in flight. Some late radial engines have torque meters incorporated in their reduction gear.

13th Annual Report, 1927

SMITH, R. H. Resistance and cooling power of various radiators. Report 261 in NACA, *13th Annual Report, 1927* (1928), pp. 163–176, illus., graph and tab. data. bibl. of 4 items.

JOACHIM, W. F., and BEARDSLEY, E. G. Factors in the design of centrifugal type injection valves for oil engines. Report 268 in NACA, *13th Annual Report, 1927* (1928), pp. 267–279, illus., graph data, bibl. of 8 items.

GARDINER, ARTHUR W., and WHEDON, WILLIAM E. The relative performance obtained with several methods of control of an over-compressed engine using gasoline. Report 272 in NACA, *13th Annual Report, 1927* (1928), pp. 329–339, drgs., diagrs., graph data, bibl. of 10 items. The German BMW and Maybach engines of 1917 were overcompressed engines, that is, the compression ratio was too high for full-throttle operation at sea level.

MARVIN, CHARLES F., JR. Combustion time in the engine cylinder and its effect on engine performance. Report 276 in NACA, *13th Annual Report, 1927* (1928), pp. 393–406, graph data.

GARDINER, ARTHUR W., and SCHEY, OSCAR W. The comparative performance of an aviation engine at normal and high inlet air temperatures. Report 277 in NACA, *13th Annual Report, 1927* (1928), pp. 409–425, graph data, bibl. of 15 items.

JOACHIM, WILLIAM F., and BEARDSLEY, EDWARD G. The effects of fuel and cylinder gas densities on the characteristics of fuel sprays for oil engines. Report 281 in NACA, *13th Annual Report, 1927* (1928), pp. 491–497, graph data, bibl. of 8 items.

14th Annual Report, 1928

JOACHIM, WILLIAM F., and KEMPER, CARLETON. The performance of several combustion chambers designed for aircraft oil engines. Report 282 in NACA, *14th Annual Report, 1927* (1928), pp. 501–510, illus., drgs., graph data, bibl. of 8 items.

WARE, MARSDEN, and SCHEY, OSCAR W. A Preliminary investigation of supercharging an air-cooled engine in flight. Report 283 in NACA, *14th Annual Report, 1928* (1929), pp. 83–91, illus., graph and tab. data, bibl. of 5 items. Aircraft used was a Navy Vought VO–1 with a Wright Aero J–4 engine.

———, and WILSON, ERNEST E. The comparative performance of Roots type aircraft engine superchargers as affected by charge in impeller speed and displacement. Report 284 in NACA, *14th Annual Report, 1928* (1929), pp. 95–106, graph and tab. data.

HICKS, CHESTER W. The measurement of maximum cylinder pressures. Report 294 in NACA, *14th Annual Report, 1928* (1929), pp. 311–319, drgs., diagrs., graph data, bibl. of 11 items.

SCHEY, OSCAR W., and WILSON, ERNEST E. On investigation of the use of discharge valves and an intake control for improving the performance of N.A.C.A. Roots type supercharger. Report 303 in NACA, *14th Annual Report, 1928* (1929), pp. 479–485, drgs., graph data, bibl. of 4 items.

STEVENS, F. W. The gaseous explosive reaction—A study of the kinetics of composite fuels. Report 305 in NACA, *14th Annual Report, 1928* (1929), pp. 503–518, graph and tab. data, bibl. of 18 items.

15th Annual Report, 1929

WEICK, FRED E. Drag and cooling with various forms of cowling for a "Whirlwind" radial air-cooled engine. Reports 313 and 314 in NACA, *15th Annual Report, 1929* (1930), pp. 165–210, illus., drgs., diagrs., graph and tab. data, bibl. of 5 items. Basic data about the development of the NACA cowling.

JOACHIM, WILLIAM F., and ROTHROCK, A. M. Fuel vapor pressures and the relation of vapor pressure to the preparation of fuel for combustion in fuel injection engines. Report 321 in NACA, *15th Annual Report, 1929* (1930), pp. 385–395, illus., drgs., graph and tab. data, bibl. of 11 items.

SCHEY, O. W., and GOVE, W. D. The effect of supercharger capacity on engine and airplane performance. Report 327 in NACA, *15th Annual Report, 1929* (1930), pp. 519–529, graph data.

GELALLES, A. G., and ROTHROCK, A. M. Experimental and analytical determination of the motion of hydraulically operated valve stems in oil engine injection systems. Report 330 in NACA, *15th Annual Report, 1929* (1930), pp. 571–588, diagrs., graph data, bibl. of 5 items.

SCHEY, OSCAR W., and BIERMANN, ARNOLD E. The effect of cowling on cylinder temperatures and performance of a Wright J–5 engine. Report 332 in NACA, *15th Annual Report, 1929* (1930), pp. 637–656, illus., drgs., graph and tab. data, bibl. of 9 items.

16th Annual Report, 1930

STEVENS, F. W. The gaseous explosive reaction at constant pressure—the reaction order and reaction rate. Report 337 in NACA, *16th Annual Report, 1930* (1931), pp. 67–82, extensive graph and tab. data.

JOACHIM, WILLIAM F., HICKS, CHESTER W., and FOSTER, HAMPTON H. The design and development of an automatic injection valve with an annular orifice of varying area. Report 341 in NACA, *16th Annual Report, 1930* (1931), pp. 137–144, diagrs., bibl. of 9 items.

SCHEY, OSCAR W., and YOUNG, ALFRED W. Comparative flight performance with a N.A.C.A. Roots supercharger and a turbo-centrifugal supercharger. Report 355 in NACA, *16th Annual Report, 1930* (1931), pp. 503–514, illus., graph and tab. data, bibl. of 8 items. Flight tests with a DH–4M2.

PETERS, MELVILLE F., SUMMERVILLE, WAYNE L., and DAVIS, MERLIN. An investigation of the effectiveness of ignition sparks. Report 359 in NACA, *16th Annual Report, 1930* (1931), pp. 575–585, diagrs., graph and tab. data, bibl. of 10 items.

Rothrock, A. M. Pressure fluctuations in a common-rail fuel injection system. Report 363 in NACA, *16th Annual Report, 1930* (1931), pp. 671–684, diagrs., graph data, bibl. of 9 items.

17th Annual Report, 1931

Stevens, F. W. The gaseous explosive reaction—The effect of pressure on the rate of propagation of the reaction zone and upon the rate of molecular transformation. Report 372 in NACA, *17th Annual Report, 1931* (1932), pp. 175–191, illus., diagrs., graph data, bibl. of 27 items.

Gelalles, A. G. Coefficients of discharge of fuel injection nozzles for compression-ignition engines. Report 373 in NACA, *17th Annual Report, 1931* (1932), pp. 193–209, diagrs., graph data, bibl. of 9 items.

Darnell, T. H. The automotive ignition coil. Report 374 in NACA, *17th Annual Report, 1931* (1932), pp. 211–236, diagrs., extensive graph data, bibl. of 12 items.

Schey, Oscar W. The comparative performance of superchargers. Report 384 in NACA, *17th Annual Report, 1931* (1932), pp. 425–437, graph and tab. data, bibl. of 10 items. Lobe, vane, and centrifugal type compressors.

———, and Biermann, Arnold E. The effect of valve timing upon the performance of a supercharged engine at altitude and an unsupercharged engine at sea level. Report 390 in NACA, *17th Annual Report, 1931* (1932), pp. 533–543, illus., graph data, bibl. of 8 items.

Rothrock, A. M. Hydraulics of fuel injection pumps for compression-ignition engines. Report 396 in NACA, *17th Annual Report, 1931* (1932), pp. 621–664, diagrs., extensive graph and tab. data, bibl. of 33 items. Early analysis of injection-pump characteristics.

Marvin, Charles F., Jr., and Best, Robert D. Flame movement and pressure development in an engine cylinder. Report 399 in NACA, *17th Annual Report, 1931* (1932), pp. 697–706, diagrs., graph data, bibl. of 5 items. Observation of flame motion by means of multiple small windows in a cylinder head.

18th Annual Report, 1932

Rothrock, A. M. Combustion in a high-speed compression-ignition engine. Report 401 in NACA, *18th Annual Report, 1932*, (1933), pp. 63–77, graph data, bibl. of 27 items.

Gelalles, A. G. Effect of orifice length-diameter ratio on fuel sprays for compression-ignition engines. Report 402 in NACA, *18th Annual Report, 1932* (1933), pp. 79–90, illus., diagr., graph data, bibl. of 19 items.

Schey, Oscar W., and Rollin, Vern G. The effect of increased carburetor pressure on engine performance at several compression ratios. Report 404 in NACA, *18th Annual Report, 1932* (1933), pp. 113–122, illus., graph data, bibl. of 10 items.

Theodorsen, Theodore, and Freeman, Ira M. The elimination of fire hazard due to back fires. Report 409 in NACA, *18th Annual Report, 1932* (1933), pp. 211–217, illus., graph data, bibl. of 10 items.

McAvoy, William H., Schey, Oscar W., and Young, Alfred W. The effect on airplane performance of the factors that must be considered in applying low-drag cowling to radial engines. Report 414 in NACA, *18th Annual Report, 1932* (1933), pp. 259–275, many photos and diagrs., graph and tab. data, bibl. of 10 items. Tests using a Curtiss XF7C–1; discussion of other types.

WOOD, DONALD H. Tests of nacelle-propeller combinations in various positions with reference to wings: Thick wing, N.A.C.A. cowled nacelle, tractor propeller. Reports 415 and 436 in NACA, *18th Annual Report, 1932* (1933), pp. 277–304, 653–692, illus., diagrs., extensive graph and tab. data., bibl. of 5 items.

LEE, DANA W. The effect of nozzle design and operating conditions on the atomization and distribution of fuel sprays. Report 425 in NACA, *18th Annual Report, 1932* (1933), pp. 505–521, diagrs., graph and tab. data, bibl. of 20 items.

ROTHROCK, A. M. The N.A.C.A. apparatus for studying the formation and combustion of fuel sprays and the results from preliminary tests. Report 429 in NACA, *18th Annual Report, 1932* (1933), pp. 549–565, illus., diagrs., drgs., graph and tab. data, bibl. of 19 items. This apparatus provides a wealth of basic information regarding injection and combustion in diesel engines. See NACA Index for the large number of test results obtained with it.

GELALLES, A. G., and MARSH, E. T. Rates of fuel discharge as affected by the design of fuel-ignition systems for internal-combustion engines. Report 433 in NACA, *18th Annual Report, 1932* (1933), pp. 607–619, diagrs., graph data, bibl. of 10 items.

ROTHROCK, A. M., and WALDRON, C. D. Fuel vaporization and its effect on combustion in a high-speed compression-ignition engine. Report 435 in NACA, *18th Annual Report, 1932* (1933), pp. 629–651, illus., drg., graph data, bibl. of 14 items.

LEE, DANA W. Experiments on the distribution of fuel in fuel sprays. Report 438 in NACA, *18th Annual Report, 1932* (1933), pp. 703–717, illus., bibl. of 10 items.

CASTLEMAN, R. A., JR. The mechanism of atomization accompanying solid injection. Report 440 in NACA, *18th Annual Report, 1932* (1933), pp. 735–744, illus., bibl. of 22 items.

19th Annual Report, 1933

LEE, DANA W., and SPENCER, ROBERT C. Photomicrographic studies of fuel sprays. Report 454 in NACA, *19th Annual Report, 1933* (1934), pp. 215–239, illus., bibl. of 12 items.

ROTHROCK, A. M., and MARSH, E. T. Penetration and duration of fuel sprays from a pump injection system. Report 455 in NACA, *19th Annual Report, 1933* (1934), pp. 241–248, illus., graph data, bibl. of 5 items.

SONTAG, HARCOURT, and BROMBACHER, W. G. Aircraft power plant instruments. Report 466 in NACA, *19th Annual Report, 1933* (1934), pp. 447–499, numerous photos, drgs., and diagrs., bibl. of 59 items.

SPANOGLE, J. A., HICKS, C. W., and FOSTER, H. H. Increasing the air charge and scavenging the clearance volume of a compression-ignition engine. Report 469 in NACA, *19th Annual Report, 1933* (1934), pp. 525–534. diagrs., graph data, bibl. of 11 items.

SCHEY, OSCAR W., and YOUNG, ALFRED W. Performance of a fuel-injection, spark-ignition engine, using a hydrogenated safety fuel. Report 471 in NACA, *19th Annual Report, 1933* (1934), pp. 557–565, diagrs., graph and tab. data, bibl. of 5 items.

20th Annual Report, 1934

GERRISH, HAROLD C., and TESSMANN, ARTHUR M. Relation of hydrogen and methane to carbon monoxide in exhaust gases from internal combustion engines. Report 476 in NACA, *20th Annual Report, 1934* (1935), pp. 53-61, graph data, bibl. of 23 items.

ROTHROCK, A. M., and MARSH, E. G. Effect of viscosity on fuel leakage between lapped plungers and sleeves, and on the discharge from a pump-injection system. Report 477 in NACA, *20th Annual Report, 1934* (1935), pp. 63-77, diagrs., graph and tab. data, bibl. of 8 items.

———, and SPENCER, R. C. Effect of moderate air flow on the distribution of fuel sprays after injection cut-off. Report 483 in NACA, *20th Annual Report, 1934* (1935), pp. 163-183, illus., graph data, bibl. of 17 items.

MARVIN, CHARLES F., JR., CALDWELL, FRANK R., and STEELE, SYDNEY. Infra-red radiation from explosions in a spark-ignition engine. Report 486 in NACA, *20th Annual Report, 1934* (1935), pp. 223-234, diagrs., graph data, bibl. of 23 items.

BIERMANN, ARNOLD E., and PINKEL, BENJAMIN. Heat transfer from finned metal cylinders in an air stream. Report 488 in NACA, *20th Annual Report, 1934* (1935), pp. 251-270, illus., extensive graph data, bibl. of 18 items.

THEODORSEN, THEODORE, and GALALLES, A. G. Vibration response of airplane structures. Report 491 in NACA, *20th Annual Report, 1934* (1935), pp. 319-337, illus., diagrs., graph and tab. data, bibl. of 6 items. Curtiss PW-9 and Consolidated N2Y biplanes were used in the tests.

DRAPER, C. S. The physical effects of detonation in a closed cylindrical chamber. Report 493 in NACA, *20th Annual Report, 1934* (1935), pp. 361-379, diagrs., graph data, bibl. of 20 items. Pioneer basic research at Massachusetts Institute of Technology on the phenomenon of detonation in spark-ignition engines.

SPANOGLE, J. A., and WHITNEY, E. G. A description and test results of a spark-ignition and a compression-ignition 2-stroke-cycle engine. Report 495 in NACA, *20th Annual Report, 1934* (1935), pp. 395-411, illus., drgs., diagrs., graph data, bibl. of 6 items. Single-cylinder comparative tests.

CLAY, WILLIAM C. Improved airplane windshields to provide vision in stormy weather. Report 498 in NACA, *20th Annual Report, 1934* (1935), pp. 445-461, illus., drgs., diagrs., bibl. of 5 items.

21st Annual Report, 1935

SCHEY, OSCAR W., and ROLLIN, VERN G. The effect of baffles on the temperature distribution and heat-transfer coefficients of finned cylinders. Report 511 in NACA, *21st Annual Report, 1935* (1936), pp. 111-123, drgs., diagrs., bibl. of 5 items.

ROTHROCK, A. M., and COHN, MILDRED. Some factors affecting combustion in an internal-combustion engine. Report 512 in NACA, *21st Annual Report, 1935* (1936), pp. 125-141, graph and tab. data, bibl. of 15 items.

LEE, DANA, W. A comparison of fuel sprays from several types of injection nozzles. Report 520 in NACA, *21st Annual Report, 1935* (1936), pp. 251-288, extensive series of photos and diagrs., bibl. of 35 items.

Rothrock, A. M., and Waldron, C. D. Some effects of injection advance angle, engine jacket temperature, and speed on combustion in a compression-ignition engine. Report 525 in NACA, *21st Annual Report, 1935* (1936), pp. 343–357, illus., diagrs., graph data, bibl. of 13 items.

Fiock, Ernest F., and King, H. Kendall. The effect of water vapor on flame velocity in equivalent $CO-O_2$ mixtures. Report 531 in NACA, *21st Annual Report, 1935* (1936), pp. 445–450, bibl. of 4 items.

——, and Roeder, Carl H. The soap-bubble method of studying the combustion of mixtures of CO and O_2. Report 532 in NACA, *21st Annual Report, 1935* (1936), pp. 451–464, illus., graph and tab. data, bibl. of 4 items.

Rothrock, A. M., and Marsh, E. T. Distribution and regularity of injection from a multi-cylinder fuel-injection pump. Report 533 in NACA, *21st Annual Report, 1935* (1936), pp. 465–476, drgs., diagrs., graph data, bibl. of 10 items.

Gerrish, Harold C., and Foster, Hampton H. Hydrogen as an auxiliary fuel in compression-ignition engines. Report 535 in NACA, *21st Annual Report, 1935* (1936), pp. 495–510, illus., drgs., graph data, bibl. of 8 items.

22nd Annual Report, 1936

Cohn, Mildren, and Spencer, Robert C. Combustion in a bomb with a fuel-injection system. Report 544 in NACA, *22nd Annual Report, 1936* (1937), pp. 107–118, illus., diagrs., graph and tab. data, bibl. of 19 items.

Rothrock, A. M., and Waldron, C. D. Effects of air-fuel ratio on fuel spray and flame formation in a compression-ignition engine. Report 545 in NACA, *22nd Annual Report, 1936* (1937), pp. 119–127, illus., diagrs., graph data, bibl. of 9 items.

Schey, Oscar W., and Rollin, Vern G. Cooling characteristics of a 2-row radial engine. Report 550 in NACA, *22nd Annual Report, 1936* (1937), pp. 177–186, illus., diagrs., graph data, bibl. of 3 items.

Fiock, Ernest F., and Roeder, Carl H. Some effects of argon and helium upon explosions of carbon monoxide and oxygen. Report 553 in NACA, *22nd Annual Report, 1936* (1937), pp. 213–222, graph data, bibl. of 4 items.

Brevoort, M. J., and Rollin, Vern G. Air flow around finned cylinders. Report 555 in NACA, *22nd Annual Report, 1936* (1937), pp 237–249, illus., drgs., graph and tab. data, bibl. of 10 items.

Marvin, Charles F., Jr., Wharton, Armistead, and Roeder, Carl H. Further studies of flame movement and pressure development in an engine cylinder. Report 556 in NACA, *22nd Annual Report, 1936* (1937), pp. 251–263, illus., diagrs., graph data, bibl. of 11 items.

Rothrock, A. M., and Waldron, C. D. Effect of nozzle design on fuel spray and flame formation in a high-speed compression-ignition engine. Report 561 in NACA, *22nd Annual Report, 1936* (1937), pp. 327–338, illus., diagrs., graph data, bibl. of 12 items.

Lee, Dana W. Measurements of fuel distribution within sprays for fuel-injection engines. Report 565 in NACA, *22nd Annual Report, 1936* (1937), pp. 389–403, diagrs., graph and tab. data, bibl. of 13 items.

Foster, H. H. The quiescent-chamber type compression-ignition engine. Report 568 in NACA, *22nd Annual Report, 1936* (1937), pp. 429–448, illus., drgs., diagrs., graph and tab. data, bibl. of 16 items.

23rd Annual Report, 1937

MOORE, CHARLES S., and COLLINS, JOHN H., JR. Pre-chamber compression-ignition engine performance. Report 577 in NACA, *23rd Annual Report, 1937* (1938), pp. 49–68, graph and tab. data, bibl. of 18 items.

SELDEN, ROBERT F., and SPENCER, ROBERT C. Heat transfer to fuel sprays into heated gases. Report 580 in NACA, *23rd Annual Report, 1937* (1938), pp. 91–107, illus., diagrs., extensive graph and tab. data, bibl. of 30 items.

SCHEY, OSCAR W., and ELLERBROCK, HERMAN H., JR. Blower cooling of finned cylinders. Report 587 in NACA, *23rd Annual Report, 1937* (1938), pp. 269–280, drgs., diagr., graph and tab. data, bibl. of 8 items.

ROTHROCK, A. M., and WALDRON, C. D. Fuel spray and flame formation in a compression-ignition engine employing air flow. Report 588 in NACA, *23rd Annual Report, 1937* (1938), pp. 281–295, illus., drgs., diagrs., bibl. of 14 items.

THEODORSEN, THEODORE, BREVOORT, M. J., and STICKLE, GEORGE W. Full-scale tests of N.A.C.A. cowlings. Report 592 in NACA, *23rd Annual Report, 1937* (1938), pp. 361–390, illus., diagrs., graph and tab. data, bibl. of 10 items.

———, ———, and ———. Cooling of airplane engines at low air speeds. Report 593 in NACA, *23rd Annual Report, 1937* (1938), pp. 391–400, illus., diagrs., graph and tab. data, bibl. of 3 items.

———, ———, ———, and GOUGH, M. N. Full-scale tests of a new type in N.A.C.A. nose-slot cowling. Report 595 in NACA, *23rd Annual Report, 1937* (1938), pp. 439–447, illus., drgs., diagrs., graph and tab. data, bibl. of 3 items. Airplane used was a Curtiss BFC–1 fighter with a Wright SGR–1510 twin-row, 14-cylinder engine.

BREVOORT, M. J., STICKLE, GEORGE W., and ELLERBROCK, HERMAN H., JR. Cooling tests of a single-row radial engine with several N.A.C.A. cowlings. Report 596 in NACA, *23rd Annual Report, 1937* (1938), pp. 449–458, illus., diagrs., graph and tab. data, bibl. of 6 items.

24th Annual Report, 1938

PINKEL, BENJAMIN. Heat-transfer processes in air-cooled engine cylinders. Report 612 in NACA, *24th Annual Report, 1938* (1939), pp. 49–64, diagrs., graph data, bibl. of 7 items.

GERRISH, HAROLD C., and VOSS, FRED. Inter-relation of exhaust-gas constituents. Report 616 in NACA, *24th Annual Report, 1938* (1939), pp. 139–146, graph data, bibl. of 9 items.

SELDEN, ROBERT F. Auto-ignition and combustion of diesel fuel in a constant-volume bomb. Report 617 in NACA, *24th Annual Report, 1938* (1939), pp. 147–159, illus., drgs., graph and tab. data, bibl. of 30 items.

ROTHROCK, A. M., and SPENCER, R. C. A photographic study of combustion and knock in a spark-ignition engine. Report 622 in NACA, *24th Annual Report, 1938* (1939), pp. 213–233, many photos, diagrs., bibl. of 22 items. Based on very high speed moving pictures through transparent windows in cylinder head. A pioneering work.

25th Annual Report, 1939

SCHEY, OSCAR W., PINKEL, BENJAMIN, and ELLERBROCK, HERMAN H., JR. Correction of temperatures of air-cooled engine cylinders for variation in engine and cooling conditions. Report 645 in NACA, *25th Annual Report, 1939* (1940), pp. 49–72, illus., diagrs., graph and tab. data, bibl. of 7 items.

LEE, DANA W. A study of air flow in an engine cylinder. Report 653 in NACA, *25th Annual Report, 1939* (1940), pp. 227–239, illus., drgs., diagrs., graph data, bibl. of 3 items.

ROTHROCK, A. M., and BIERMANN, ARNOLD E. The knocking characteristics of fuels in relation to maximum permissible performance of aircraft engines. Report 655 in NACA, *25th Annual Report, 1939* (1940), pp. 267–288, graph data, bibl. of 20 items. Important contribution.

———, and SPENCER, R. C. The influence of directed air flow on combustion in a spark-ignition engine. Report 657 in NACA, *25th Annual Report, 1939* (1940), pp. 313–326, illus., diagrs., bibl. of 15 items.

STICKLE, GEORGE W. Design of N.A.C.A. cowlings for radial air-cooled engines. Report 662 in NACA, *25th Annual Report, 1939* (1940), pp. 383–393, illus., drgs., diagrs., bibl. of 8 items,

www.ingramcontent.com/pod-product-compliance
Lightning Source LLC
Chambersburg PA
CBHW080513110426
42742CB00017B/3103